I held hope in my hands that day, performing CPR, but survival seemed medically impossible after 45 minutes without a heartbeat. And yet, he is here. Reading this book took me back to that sacred space between life and death- and reminded me that God does indeed perform miracles. This is more than a story of survival – it is a testimony to the power of prayer, the strength of community, and a God that never gives up on us. This story forever changed me, and I believe it will change you too.

—Joye Feinzig

I believed in what I could explain - until I couldn't. These 45 days changed everything. This book turned a skeptic into a believer and stands as living proof that God performs miracles and that prayer has power.

—Jack Feinzig

We have never prayed for anything as fervently as we did for Kevin. From the gut-wrenching image of Amy pleading with paramedics to the impossible reality of Kevin waking from a month-long coma without brain damage, this story is breathtaking. It is a captivating journey from utter devastation to a stunning example of God's grace in action. A must-read for anyone who needs to believe in miracles again.

—Steve and Janet Wright

Ever wonder if miracles exist today? Does supernatural intervention—unexplainable phenomena—happen in modern times? Is there a reason you're still breathing in and out? If you've ever been curious or wrestled with these questions, Kevin's story is a must-read. Through the power of persistent prayer and bold acts of faith, this true story reveals profound divine truths. Unquestionably, there is a marked purpose on every human life.

—Liz Rollins

Having known Kevin for over 25 years, I can say he has always been the kind of guy whose exuberant energy and joyful spirit light up every room he walks into. To go from that to watching him fight for his life on life support for weeks was utterly heartbreaking. But this book isn't just about the sadness, it's a God centered testimony of what happens when a family refuses to let go of their faith in Christ and His power in their lives. Seeing Amy's unshakeable trust in the Lord during those long weeks was true resilience and hope. If you've ever doubted whether God still does the impossible, you need to read Kevin and Amy's story. It is a beautiful account of a real miracle that will leave you completely inspired.

—Juliet Hanak

Kevin's story of healing and restoration continues to feed my ministry and inspire others…especially me. From praying for him in ICU to seeing him lead other men and families in the church, his journey has been one of faith and commitment. This book shares that story with depth and honesty. 2 Timothy 1:7 tells us…"For God has not given us a spirit of fear, but of power and of love and of a sound mind." Kevin's story is a testament to this passage.

—Brian Lewis, Men's Ministry Pastor: Seacoast Church

When Kevin Strader suffered a massive heart attack and we all thought we had lost him, I stood in that hospital with his wife Amy and watched God do what only He can do - bring hope where there was none. In 45 Days, Kevin thoughtfully and honestly reflects on that miracle with the steady mind of an engineer and the humble faith of a man who has wrestled with where God was in the darkest moments. This book strengthened my faith as a pastor, and it will challenge and encourage anyone who reads it.

—Josh Surratt, Lead Pastor of Seacoast Church

Thank you Kevin for putting your story down on paper! I was there I witnessed it, you are a true miracle from God and the individual segments give credibility to Gods hand! For anyone who is seeking, hope, healing or confirmation I encourage you to read and enjoy the story!

—Sam Lesky, Executive Pastor of Campus
Operations: Seacoast Church

I have had the privilege and honor of knowing Kevin for many years. I so appreciate how he has grown as a Man of God, a loving husband & father, & a committed friend to the many who have crossed his path. His story is one of perseverance, of encouragement, and of healing as it is an incredible example of a man of integrity seeking to make a difference of eternal significance in touching other lives with the desire to give them hope and peace with the battles of life they are facing.

—Michael Morris, LPC & Pastor, The
Counseling Center of Seacoast

Kevin's story is a powerful testimony of a near-death experience that reshaped his understanding of himself and deepened his faith in God. As he fought for life, those around him—especially his wife and children—stood close, praying fervently for his recovery. The experience not only transformed Kevin, but also deeply impacted those who surrounded him in faith and prayer. His journey is a moving reminder of the power of faith, family, and community in life's most fragile moments.

—Janet Koenig

To watch Kevin and Amy put all of their faith into trusting our Lord during these events and the miracle that our Lord performed is truly beautiful and inspiring!

—Dan Biggerstaff

Although it was a very difficult time, seeing how God aligned all of the circumstances to completely heal Kevin and strengthen Amy was a transformative experience. God allowed a situation where only He could receive the Glory for this miraculous healing, and we were amazed and blessed to witness His glory unfold in real time.

—Patty Biggerstaff

Kevin's story is a powerful reminder miracles often unfold one step at a time. After a devastating heart event nearly taking his life, what followed was a journey marked by grace, perseverance and unwavering prayers of family, friends, and community. This book beautifully captures not only Kevin's fight to live, but the countless moments along the way feeling nothing short of miraculous. Today as we watch him live and thrive, his story has become something we celebrate together, a testimony deepening our faith and reminding us of the strength found in hope, love and God's presence through every trial we face.

—Jim Koenig

45 DAYS

FAITH, LOVE, AND
PRAYERS

KEVIN R. STRADER

This book is dedicated to the following:

To my wife: You love me unconditionally, sacrifice unselfishly and fought courageously to save my life here on Earth. You are a true inspiration. I love you.

To my daughters: You have endured so much. You showed tremendous courage through it all. I pray for God's blessing and protection for both of you. I love you.

To those who prayed and supported our family: Thank you

CONTENTS

FOREWORD

On Dec 7, 2021, my life changed in "the blink of an eye" when my husband had a sudden cardiac arrest in our home. I watched my unconscious husband be carried out of our home on a stretcher. In that moment, I realized how precious and fleeting life can be. As I listened to our girls sob that night, I was nearly broken. As his body swelled with fluid, I felt the warmth of his hand and wished for his hand to squeeze mine. I saw him fail his neurological checks. I ached to hear his voice. Words cannot express how difficult the journey was. My faith sustained me during the toughest days. I felt a resolve in my heart and mind to have hope as long as Kevin was alive. I prayed for a miracle. I was determined to stand in the gap for my husband and storm the gates of Heaven. I experienced all the bad days when there looked to be no hope, but I also got a front row seat to a modern-day miracle and the goodness of God. God performed a miracle in Kevin, and it was more than just keeping him with our family. The miracle spoke life in our faith, made believers out of unbelievers, and showed medical staff and believers that God still performs miracles.
To God be the Glory!

Amy Strader

INTRODUCTION

When I was a kid growing up in Lynchburg, Virginia, I spent many afternoons playing basketball in our driveway or practicing baseball fielding skills by bouncing tennis balls off the cinderblock walls of our basement, all the while dreaming of becoming a Major League Baseball player. If I couldn't achieve that, I thought it would be cool to become a firefighter or maybe a paramedic. I never once thought I would grow up to write a book and I certainly never thought a firefighter or a paramedic would save my life. But here we are.

I do not claim to be a professional writer—please keep that in mind. I am an engineer by trade, which means I can barely speak the English language, much less write using it. But I can run circles around you with math problems and I am a very efficient problem solver. So, why did I write this book? I was compelled to tell my story. A story of a tragic event that turned into a remarkable response by a community. A community of neighbors, first responders, health care professionals, friends, believers, and non-believers who all came together to save my life here on earth.

A friend asked me who my target audience is for this book. At the time, I responded that I wasn't sure. I just wanted to be obedient to the calling of writing my story. That part is true; however, I knew exactly who I wrote this book for.

For the individual who is looking for strength, peace, and hope in a world that just doesn't make sense, this book was written for you. You may be looking for answers and just cannot seem to reconcile them in a very chaotic world. You found this book somehow, and I want to speak to you through its words. Please don't shy away from reading, instead, walk through this journey with open eyes and an open heart. As you read, think about all that happened and contemplate the probability that I survived the events that unfolded. At the end, you can decide if all of this is a random act or if the probabilities are so great that there must be something else to this.

This book is also for the individual who is discouraged in your faith or who has experienced tragic events. My family has endured a number of tragic events that do not make sense. So, I can relate. I encourage you, however, to walk through this story with me and see if your life isn't changed in the end.

This story is about faith, love, and prayers. It's about a community that responded to save my life and support my family during this tragic event. It's about my wife who had the strength and fortitude to orchestrate the response. It's about a community that rallied and prayed for my survival. The real story though is how my survival and recovery has impacted other people's lives—their faith, their belief, and their hope.

It is my prayer that this story will change your life, give you hope, increase your faith, and strengthen your belief that life is not just a random act. Your life is so much more. It is intentional and you have a Creator who wants nothing more than to walk with you on this journey called life. May this story be a blessing to you and may you be forever changed.

1

JUST AN ORDINARY DUDE

For the most part, I am pretty ordinary. Not famous. Not real popular. I live an ordinary middle-class life with a home in the suburbs in our town of 30 years. I've been happily married to my wife, Amy, for 32 years, and we've raised two daughters. I've worked for one company most of those years. We've regularly attended the same church for many years, where I have volunteered and become part of a community. But, life gets busy with kids and work and I had to pull back on church involvement. I exercise on an inconsistent basis, with spurts of being motivated to work out at home or at the gym. I enjoy sports—basketball, softball, and racquet sports—but injuries stopped me from playing for a period of time, and then, I'm back to inconsistent work outs. Does any of this sound familiar?

In general, my health is good. I maintain a decent body weight, blood pressure, and important blood values like cholesterol and triglycerides. At times though, I skirt on the edge of admonishment from my doctor.

But this is where I break from the ordinary middle-class dude. The last 12 years have had its not-so-normal challenges, filled with tragedies, heartbreaks, stress, chaos, and confusion, but also triumph.

In the summer of 2013, my oldest brother, Wally, started to have headaches for days at a time. Doctors discovered a brain aneurysm that was actively leaking. Years earlier, my mother's sister had died from a ruptured aneurysm, so we were well aware of the severity of the situation. Obviously, this was stressful for our whole family and we all descended on the hospital in Virginia while my brother had emergency surgery. Fortunately, he survived.

The next year, my youngest daughter, Caroline, started to have severe headaches. We ruled out the normal culprits like a sinus infection, but her headaches continued. With my brother's diagnoses fresh in our minds, we had her scanned and doctors identified a small aneurysm. Amy called me with the news while I was on a business trip. As you can imagine, I was distraught and immediately flew home. Our conversation with the neurosurgeon revealed that it was not an emergency, but it eventually would need to be fixed. With our family history, he also recommended that my oldest daughter, Reagan, and myself should get scanned. Fortunately, Reagan was free and clear. However, I was not, I too had an aneurysm. The doctor was more concerned about mine and recommended it be repaired soon.

We scheduled both mine and Caroline's surgeries for July 2014. Mine was on a Monday and hers on Wednesday of that same week. I wanted to go first. I told the neurosurgeon that if he was going to have a mishap, I wanted it to be on me, not my daughter. I also thought if I went first, it would help Caroline with any anxiety she may have. My parents and my brother, Wally, who had surgery the prior year would be there to support Amy.

My surgery went off without a hitch. It lasted about an hour and the aneurysm was coiled successfully. I spent one night in the hospital and was able to return with my family on Wednesday for Caroline's surgery. We all joined her in the pre-op area to pray before surgery. Her surgery was similar to mine in terms of complexity and should only take about an hour. After she was wheeled back to the operating room, our family moved to the waiting area.

At first, we sat and tried to be calm. But, I got antsy and periodically walked the halls. As it got closer to the hour, I walked more. Then, I prayed. In my spirit, I was concerned. I felt like I needed to respond. I found a quiet part of the hallway and prayed. *God, lead and direct the surgeons, and let Caroline be okay.* An hour and fifteen minutes came, no updates. More praying, more walking. Something was different than my surgery and I started to worry.

Then, around the corner, I saw doctors dash to an elevator. They looked anxious. They saw us, but didn't say anything. They didn't want to. I got down on my knees and prayed like I had never prayed before.

At these times, there are no levers I can pull to fix something. As an engineer, I am a problem solver. When a problem comes, I immediately make a plan to rectify the issue. Then I work the plan. But with this, there is no plan I can work. From a material, earthly perspective, I am helpless. I can only work on the things in my control, but when it comes to things outside my control, there is only one thing I can do—pray.

That can be difficult, especially for a "fixer." However, I recognize that in certain circumstances, I have to come to grips with my limitations as a human and look for strength from other places. In my case, my strength comes from God.

An hour and forty-five minutes passed. I stood in the hallway and out of the corner of my eye, I saw Caroline being wheeled to the recovery area. Shortly after, the surgeon explained that one of the coils came partially dislodged and a stent had to be inserted to hold it in place. She would be fine. To say the weight of the world was removed from my soul would be an understatement.

Later that year, two days prior to Thanksgiving, I received a call from my father. My mother had been rushed to the emergency room. She had been sitting in her chair on the phone with her sister, as well as talking to my father, when she started exhibiting signs of a stroke.

I immediately got in my car and rushed to Raleigh, North Carolina to be with my parents and Wally. Once I arrived, I learned that my mother had suffered a brain hemorrhage. From that day forward, her life and our family's life was altered.

The hospital staff stabilized her through the night and moved her to the Intensive Care Unit. Further tests showed that the bleed was in a part of her brain where doctors could not operate. In addition, the bleed had not fully stopped and her life was at risk.

At one point, the ICU attending physician informed my father that they had investigated everything they could to save my mother's life, and there was only one thing left to try—a clotting agent. The medication was designed to clot active bleeds in the circulatory system. The downside—it can clot where it shouldn't and cause additional strokes, and ultimately, death. With no other options, my father agreed to this possible solution.

My father was also an engineer—a problem solver. But, like myself during Caroline's surgery, he couldn't pull any levers to save my mother. He gave authority to the doctors to do what could be done; then he walked down the hallway and through a set of double doors to be alone.

All that time, I worked on the problem. I thought things would get resolved and my mother would recover. My head spun. It was hard to understand what was happening. I tried to grasp her condition and provide the necessary solution. I tried to support my father and assist where needed. I tried to keep our family informed of the situation as best as I could. But I wasn't trained for this. Maybe, if I had known months earlier, I could have read a book on how to manage this situation. But how can you anticipate these things? You can't. You just react the best that you can.

After a few moments, I found my father alone behind the double doors. I had always known him as a strong, determined individual who rarely showed emotion. But in this moment, I saw him exhibit an emotion I had only experienced with him one time before. He was propped up against a wall sobbing. The full extent of the situation had broken through and it had broken him. He did all he could for my mother and he knew he might lose her that night. And that broke him apart. I held my father in the hallway for a period of time. That was all I knew to do.

For 30 years, my parents had been a part of a Baptist church in their town, where they were actively involved in Sunday school, the choir, and committees. My father served as a deacon. They had deep relationships with a number of people who responded in full force. They showed up at the hospital to support my parents, and most importantly, to pray for my mother.

That evening, a group of women from church visited her room and surrounded my mother in prayer and song. It was as if God sent angels to minister to her and to comfort her, and the rest of us. While the ladies prayed and sang, my mother did something that she would never do again, she raised her left arm. It gave me a glimmer of hope for recovery, but now I recognize that it was a sign of worship.

My mother survived the event initially, but the hemorrhage caused her to be paralyzed on the left side of her body for the remainder of her life. She spent over a month in the hospital and then three months in a rehab hospital. During that time, numerous people from church stepped up. Many went to the facilities to sit with her. Others spent time with my father. Meals were brought. Prayers were sent up. People just wanted to help. We were uncertain of what the future held, but we knew that they had the support of a community.

In April 2015, my mother returned home, where she received in-home care twenty-four hours a day, seven days a week, for the next four years. Fortunately, during those years, she had her mind and could communicate with us. But it had to have been depressing for her. Most of the things she enjoyed had been taken away. Her love of gardening and cooking, singing in the choir, attending Sunday school, volunteering at church, and traveling to see family—all gone. But she rarely showed sorrow. She stayed true to being a mother and she did her best to protect me from her struggles.

My brothers and I, and our families, supported my parents as often as we could. Each of us lived long distance, but we planned visits that often revolved around helping with doctor's appointments or working around their house. Every year we made time for a family Christmas.

Then, my father started having health issues. He was diagnosed with multiple myeloma after suffering a vertebra fracture while helping my mother move in her bed. Over the next four years, he endured four more vertebrae fractures. This disease took a toll on his body—particularly his kidneys.

My parent's lives became a moving target. Just like that, they both needed help. I often received lengthy phone calls from the in-home care company or my father. I had to drive several four-and-a-half-hour trips to their house to resolve care issues. Fortunately, remote work is a blessing, but being separated from my wife and daughters is not. It was a balance.

I helped my parents as best as I could and relied on Amy to keep our family running while I was gone. But we both had to keep up with our jobs, and Amy, too, was caring for her own mother. Numerous times I wished we lived closer to my parents, but we all adapted and did the best we could under the circumstances.

2

LOSSES

Four years had passed since my brother Wally's aneurysm had been repaired. In late 2017, it was determined that he would need additional coiling to further stabilize it. I wasn't worried, we had been here before. We gathered for Christmas at my parent's house and spoke briefly of his upcoming surgery. He lived near my aunt in Virginia, and she would be with him at the hospital, so I didn't plan to be there. As we wrapped up our Christmas visit, I gave him a hug—rare for me. Little did I know, it would be one of our last hugs.

In early January 2018, my brother went into surgery. After the coils were placed, a stent was to be placed over the coils to hold them in place. However, a medical device failure resulted in the stent being deployed too soon and out of place. To fix it, the doctor placed a second stent to cover the coiled area. However, he made a critical mistake. The second stent was placed over the pathway of a major artery. My brother's condition was monitored closely, and blood thinner was continually added to his body to prevent clots. Unfortunately, this solution did not work and my brother incurred a major stroke.

As soon as I heard the news, I drove to Raleigh to pick up my father and continued on to the hospital in Virginia. Seeing

Wally in this condition was heart breaking. He lay there in bed, motionless and unaware of his surroundings. My head spun...again. I had vivid flashbacks to when my mother was in the hospital.

Again, I started in on the problem. *There must be a solution.* We asked for a full explanation of what had happened—a time-line and a drawing of the arteries where the stents were placed.

After seeing the drawing, I knew how deathly severe the situation was. My brother would not recover and probably not survive. I begged for an intervention and made my own suggestions—maybe cut a hole in the stent to allow more blood flow. The doctors refused and stated that it would only make things worse.

I was unhinged. Furious beyond comprehension. Even today, seven years later, I get worked up. In my mind, it was by far the biggest medical failure I have heard of, and for that, it is a really hard situation to get past. My brother laid in a state where, in my mind, the doctors had given up. My father was devastated. We had already been through so much with my mother, and now here we were again. But this time, we were dealing with a lack of response from the medical team. It was unfathomable. It took everything in me not to completely explode.

My father and I stayed at Wally's home while we processed next steps in his care. One early morning, my father received a call from a surgeon at the hospital. Due to the stroke, my brother's brain had swelled, and to save his life a portion of his skull would need to be cut out to allow the brain to expand and alleviate the pressure.

It was dark outside as we sat in my brother's living room and tried to process what we'd just been told. There was only one answer—proceed with the intervention. It felt like another gut punch to an already worn out gut. My father sat there with his head in his hands trying to make sense of it all.

Wally survived the weekend, but remained in a critical state. Meanwhile, my father and I met with palliative care to talk through what life would be like for my brother if he were able to leave the hospital. With so many unknowns, it was hard to make plans.

Over the next couple of weeks, Wally became more alert and responsive, but he was never able to speak. When I visited him, I would talk to him and look for any response. I still remember looking in his eyes. It was the only doorway I had to his soul. I knew he could hear me and probably understand me. *What was he thinking? What did he feel? How was he dealing with all this?* Those answers remain a mystery.

My other brother, Stephen, visited as well and I returned home for a couple of weeks. We continued our discussions on what Wally's care would look like going forward. But on February 5, Wally suffered a second, more devastating stroke. Though he initially survived, it would ultimately end his life.

Once I received the news of his stroke, I traveled to Raleigh the next day to pick up my parents before we drove to Virginia to see my brother. I wheeled my mother into the ICU to see her son alive for the last time. Though he was now unresponsive, she sat next to him in her wheelchair and told him over and over and over again how much she loved him. Heartbreaking does not even describe the scene.

I drove my mother back home to Raleigh and then returned to the hospital the next day with my father. We asked more questions of the medical staff to ensure that nothing else could be done. Then on February 9, we agreed to withdraw care and take my brother off life support. I sat there and looked at Wally's lifeless body and saw my father's hand in his. My brother passed the next day. Devastated does not begin to describe how I felt in that moment.

At his funeral the next week, the sound of a bugle echoed down the hill to us. Taps was played and it was as if every part of my insides were being ripped out. My brother was a Navy veteran, just like my father. It is an honor to have a brother who was a veteran and incredible to have the military honor my brother in that way. As we sat at the gravesite, the honor guard respectfully folded the American flag and handed it to my mother.

How could God allow something like this to occur? My brother was a believer, a devoted deacon in his church, and a good person. My parents, the same. *How could this have happened to him, to them? And all of us? Where was God in all of this?*

The next couple of months were tough on everyone. Stephen, his wife, Amy, and I began the process of cleaning out Wally's home, while my parents dealt with the loss of their oldest son. My family grieved while we were distracted with work, school, and college applications for my oldest daughter, Reagan. I didn't know it for another year, but I am certain I went through a period of depression in the months following my brother's death.

But, the year went on, and we transitioned into a new phase. Reagan graduated from high school and began her college career. That same fall, I started a new role within my company that would take me to Iraq in February of 2019. It was a big transition for my family. I would be away from home more often and wouldn't be able to share the family responsibilities as much as before.

Life seemed to move forward, but we could not have anticipated what was coming in the following years—more heartbreak, stress, chaos, and confusion.

3

MORE LOSSES

In February of 2019, I prepared for my new assignment in Iraq. Before I could leave, I had to fill out forms, complete physicals, and buy supplies. I also visited Reagan at college and stopped to see my parents and in-laws.

The first four-week rotation at the Rumaila Oil Field in Southern Iraq began in February. It was fascinating. The complex where I worked and lived employed people from 70 different countries, all with different religions and cultural backgrounds.

While there, I worked seven days a week for four weeks. Then, I could return home to the States for four weeks. When I was home, I was off work before I returned to Iraq for another four weeks. It was a tight knit community and I developed great working relationships and personal friendships. We worked together, ate together, worked out, and played sports together. It was incredible. My first rotation ended in mid-March, and I returned home to my family.

Two days after I arrived home, I received a phone call from my father. My mother had incurred a second stroke and had been rushed to the hospital. It was bad. Just like many times before, I packed up and drove up to Raleigh.

When I got to the hospital, my mother was unresponsive in the ICU. My father was by her bedside. I was transported back to the prior year in a similar room with my father and in a similar situation with my brother. The doctors gave us the same prognosis they had given for my brother—my mother would not recover.

When doctors give you this information, it is not only hard news to take, but it is hard to decipher. It is a fruitless venture to try to solve the problem, but, I digested the information and quizzed the doctor. Just like with my brother, I wanted to see pictures—proof of the diagnosis. But, when I was faced with the facts, I felt helpless.

I had watched my father navigate the muddy waters with my brother, and once again, I watched him. We digested the same information and we were given the same prognosis. He would, however, take his time. He was in no rush to let my mother go. And why should he? They had been married for over 58 years. He had cared for her with 24/7 assistance for over four years. He had sacrificed a lot for her care, including his own health.

I have often said that during those four years, I had never met anyone who exhibited the qualities of Jesus like my father did. He sacrificed, and served, and was 100 percent committed to her. It was a hard four years for both of them, but he was an example of how you should sacrifice and serve those you love...just like Jesus.

Over the next couple of days, we monitored my mother's health and looked for signs of improvement. Friends visited to pray for her and encourage us. The support of their church friends was tremendous during a really tough time.

After a few days, my father came to peace and let me know it was time. We had been through this together with my brother and I was prepared to go through it again. This time, I watched my father hold my mother's hand until she slipped into Heaven.

It is hard to explain all the emotions a person feels in that moment. You are sitting in front of a loved one, one whom you have known your whole life. One whom you have shared so much with. And now, that loved one is gone. There is no coming back. When a loved one is gone, they are gone forever. You feel this in that moment. As you gaze upon their lifeless body, all the memories flood in and it is really hard to process. Knowing that my mother was a believer is comforting, but my soul still aches. It doesn't comprehend Heaven, so it hurts and hurts and hurts.

The following weekend, we held her funeral. We got through it, just like with my brother's funeral. But this time my father returned to his home alone. I returned to Iraq and we started the process of moving forward again. Amy started a new routine of calling my father every day—one they both enjoyed. They formed a strong bond over the next few years.

As the summer of 2019 approached, I received a phone call from Amy while I was in Iraq with more bad news. Her younger sister, Allison, was diagnosed with stage 4 metastatic breast cancer. She lived twelve hours away from us and was a single mother to her five-year-old daughter, Sarah. Allison seemed to take the news well and was very optimistic. Amy and I began making adjustments to assist her, starting with taking Allison and Sarah on a vacation to lift their spirits. Afterward, Amy routinely visited Kentucky to help with doctor's appointments and to help Allison keep up with life's demands.

In August of 2019, I received another tough phone call while I was in Iraq. Amy's mother, who had battled several physical ailments through the years had fallen sick. My wife had taken her to the Medical University of South Carolina

(MUSC) Emergency Room in Charleston. Amy was distraught. I prayed for her and for my mother-in-law and tried to be strong while working half way around the world. Once again, very little was in my control. Thoughts dominated my mind. *This was not sounding good.* All I could do was find a private space and pray.

A few hours after her initial call, my wife called to tell me that her mother—her best friend—had passed away. And I wasn't there to comfort her. Amy was by her mother's side as she slipped off to Heaven. I knew the pain of that moment well.

My company flew me home the next day to be with my family. Once again, Amy and our girls were processing the loss of a mother and a grandmother. We held her funeral the next week before I returned to another four-week rotation in Iraq where I would continue to work rotations throughout the year.

On January 3, 2020, President Donald Trump ordered a drone strike that killed Iranian General Qasem Soleimani near the Baghdad airport. For our safety, my company removed all United States personnel from Iraq. Professionally, this was devastating. I lost a job that I loved and had to leave the people and the experience. Now I had the additional stress of trying to secure another job within my company or find something else.

One job option was a move to Houston, but at the time, my daughter, Caroline, was a junior in high school and we were not crazy about a possible move. A move to Texas would have also impacted Amy's ability to help Allison in Kentucky on a regular basis. Fortunately, I secured a job within my company that allowed me to remain in Charleston. This was a huge relief which alleviated additional stress.

Then, March 2020. Lockdowns, masks, and isolation caused more stress, confusion, and chaos. Our girls were now home taking online classes and we all tried to make sense of this new rhythm. Amy took more frequent trips to Kentucky to help with Allison's deteriorating health. But her older sister and her cousin, Teresa, stepped in to reduce the number of trips she needed to take. With our girls home and a knee surgery for me, we were so grateful for the extra hands.

Reagan returned to college in 2021, just in time for us to start another round of college applications, campus visits, and college selections for Caroline, who graduated high school that spring.

My sister-in-law battled cancer valiantly, but it became too difficult for her to live on her own and raise her then seven-year-old daughter. So in July of 2021, Allison and Sarah moved to South Carolina to live with us. Although it was the right move, it brought a tremendous amount of stress that we had not considered in our eagerness to help. Their lifestyle was vastly different than ours and initially, blending our families made for a stressful situation.

Amy and I were listed as guardians of Sarah in the event Allison passed, but we were uncertain if we were the right choice for Sarah long-term. Other options within the family existed, but Allison was not interested in exploring them. She remained optimistic about her prognosis even though the reality of her disease did not look good.

On October 4, Allison experienced severe abdominal pain—the cancer had spread to her liver. Amy took her to the hospital where doctors attempted an operation to relieve the symptoms. But Allison's liver was too compromised and there was nothing they could do. Family members visited her in the hospital for the last time and we brought Sarah into her mother's hospital room to say goodbye. On October 9, with Amy by her side, Allison lost her battle and went to Heaven.

Over the course of three and a half years, our family endured four funerals. As I write this book, we have lost two more loved ones—my father and my father-in-law passed away in the first half of 2023. That's six close family members in five years. Unprecedented and hard to take.

In the two months that followed the loss of Allison, we began to recover and help Sarah transition into a new life with us as her guardians. We, mainly Amy, established a routine for Sarah and got her involved in several activities like gymnastics, swimming lessons, and piano lessons. I taught Sarah how to ride a bike and we became involved in her school activities. We were standing in the gap for her mother who left us too soon.

During that transition, Amy noticed a large lump in the front of her neck and experienced issues with her voice and swallowing. After a few consultations with local doctors, she decided to see a specialist in Tampa, Florida. In early November of 2021, Amy had surgery to remove a cancerous portion of her thyroid. Once again, Amy's cousin Teresa stepped in to help with Sarah, as both of our daughters were in college. With no surgery complications, we returned home and settled in, ready to make a new life for ourselves and for Sarah.

Then on December 7, life changed again.

4

CHAOS

In the early morning hours of December 7, 2021, I clamored vigorously through the bedroom closet in search of our blood pressure machine. I wasn't feeling well. The ruckus of my search woke Amy, who got out of bed to help me find the machine. I do not remember anything else about that morning—or much of the days leading up to that morning.

What I am about to convey is direct information from Amy and our neighbor, Joye:

When Amy arrived at the closet to help me find the machine, I was clearly agitated. This behavior was a bit out of character for me, especially that early in the morning. My blood pressure was high—also abnormal for me. I took it again, a bit lower, but still high. I laid back down and fell asleep. Amy checked on me regularly as I slept peacefully for a couple of hours.

While I rested, Amy started to get concerned and began to research signs of a heart attack. I wasn't showing signs of distress and I had settled down to where she felt comfortable leaving the house to take our niece, Sarah, to school. After school drop off, Amy made a stop at the grocery store for two items. She was quick, aided by the fact that she did not run into anyone she knew, which ended up being a godsend. While she was gone, I awakened, ate breakfast, and made my way to our back porch.

Amy returned home and checked on me. I complained of aches in my jaw and left arm. She insisted that we go to the ER. Initially, I resisted. *It wasn't a serious issue. I was healthy.* The thought of a major medical emergency was far from my mind. However, I agreed to go to the hospital. Amy used the restroom and got ready to leave. I walked to our bathroom.

A loud gasp and a thud.

Amy rushed to our bathroom where she found me lying on my back, hands clutched to my chest, and my pupils fixed. I gasped for air and started to turn blue. As you can imagine, Amy was stunned. But in that moment, she heard God speak to her, "If you do not get it together, you are going to lose him."

Amy sprang into action and she fought for my life. She gave me a few breaths to stop my gasps. She then called our neighbor, Joye, a nurse, to describe the situation. Without hesitation, Joye sprinted across our yards and into our home while her husband, Jack, called 911.

Joye entered the bathroom and saw me on the floor. My condition was much worse than she expected—unconscious, unresponsive, pulseless, and not breathing. I had turned a shade of blue that she had never seen before. Joye immediately began life-saving CPR and continued until the paramedics arrived. While on the phone with the 911 call center ladies, Amy held my feet and cried.

Joye could not believe what was happening. She knew me as a vibrant, healthy, friendly neighbor. Now with every push on my chest, she heard ribs crack and cartilage pop. She heard fluid in my lungs caused by the aspiration of vomit when I collapsed—which prevented her breaths from filling my lungs. Every second was horrible. Even if she could establish a heartbeat, she felt it wouldn't matter because of the fluid in my lungs. Sirens in the distance came as a welcome relief.

The first paramedic arrived within four minutes, with two more right behind him. When the third paramedic arrived, Joye backed away from me to be with Amy right outside of our bedroom door. Within a few minutes, our bathroom and bedroom were filled with paramedics and firefighters, who worked diligently to save my life on earth.

My heart was in ventricular fibrillation—one of the most lethal heart rhythms that exist. It can claim your life within minutes. Over the next 45 minutes, paramedics injected epi-nephrine and amiodarone, and administered defibrillator shocks to my heart in an attempt to restart it and restore a normal rhythm.

As each shock was administered, Amy cried while Joye listened and hoped to hear that a normal heartbeat had been established. The first shock was delivered...no pulse. The second shock...no pulse. The third and fourth...still no pulse. The paramedics emptied their tackle boxes and used every meth-od they had. Amy pleaded with them to not give up. I cannot imagine what my wife must have felt in those moments. She certainly could not have imagined that the morning would turn out that way. Joye, full of encouragement, hugged my wife, but she began to wonder what life would be like for Amy, our girls, and our niece without me.

Hope faded. Fifth shock...no pulse.

Joye clasped Amy's hand and told her, "The only thing to do now is pray." They both kneeled and prayed. In that mo-ment, paramedics delivered a sixth defibrillator shock. Joye, who had begun to lose hope moments ago, heard a different sound from the defibrillator. "Amy, I think they have a pulse."

After 45 minutes of tremendous effort from Joye, several

paramedics and firemen, six defibrillator shocks, and two people on their knees begging God for a miracle—a normal pulse was established. There was hope.

I was placed on a gurney and carried to the ambulance. At that time, Joye wondered if this was the last time I would leave my home. I had been without a regular heartbeat for 45 minutes. Her medical training made her think that my condition was irreversible and all this effort was just to give Amy and our girls time to say goodbye. Joye, who is very analytical, didn't believe I would survive and, if I did, she feared I might be disabled or in a vegetative state for the rest of my life. She even felt guilty, wondering if her efforts to save me helped my family, or just prolonged their suffering.

Although a good hospital is located across the street from our house, Amy gave permission for a twenty-five minute drive to MUSC, where they are better equipped to treat this condition. Before the ambulance pulled away, Amy asked a paramedic if I would be ok. He responded, "Let's just take it one step at a time." He probably didn't think I would survive. He stayed at the house after everyone left to answer Amy's questions and ensure she would know exactly where to find me.

It just did not make sense that I survived. There could only be one reason.

5

UNCERTAINTY

Amy was rattled. She struggled to gather her keys and phone before leaving for the hospital. Joye and Jack made sure the house was secured. Jack was fantastic and drove Amy straight to the hospital. Shaken, Amy could not have handled the traffic, traffic lights, and morning chaos that ensues on Highway 17.

On the way, Amy texted friends and family to tell them the news. Their responses of prayer and support had a snowball effect throughout the day and into the weeks to come.

Jack dropped Amy off at the MUSC Chest Pain Center/Cardiac ER at the Ashley River Tower (ART) building. Within minutes of checking in at reception, she was escorted to the hallway right outside my room. From there, she could see a room full of hospital staff working hard to save my life. The ER doctor asked Amy questions and informed her that I had a seizure in the ER before she arrived. The medical team wasn't sure if my near-death experience was caused by a stroke or a heart attack. Amy's first-hand account would be vital information for their diagnosis and treatment.

She explained my symptoms before and after she found me on the bathroom floor. While she spoke with them, doctors attempted to clear fluid from my lungs so I could breathe. Ultimately, they decided to intubate me. Doctors and nurses worked hard to stabilize me as much as possible. The next steps would be crucial to my survival.

With the information Amy and the paramedics provided, doctors sent me to the heart cath lab to look for blockages that might require an intervention—no blockages were found. Amy wasn't allowed to see me, so they sent her to the Cardiac ICU waiting room.

Word spread. Within a couple of hours, Amy was not alone. Her friend Liz was the first person to arrive to the hospital and met Amy at the ICU waiting room. Amy's cousin, Teresa, dropped everything she was doing, packed up, and drove three hours to Charleston. She knew her job well—take care of Sarah. Other friends, Janet, Patty, and Kellye arrived later in the day and took on different roles to help Amy. Jim, Mark, and Dirk also supported her later that day.

Amy contacted Pastor Michael Morris from our church. He was in a meeting with other pastors, and they wrapped up their meeting to come to the hospital. Pastors Josh Surratt and Sam Lesky also arrived that afternoon. Amy didn't have a lot of information about my condition at that time, but everyone offered support any way they could.

I cannot imagine what the next phone calls were like for Amy—telling our girls about their dad's condition. Since they were not nearby, I'm sure they felt helpless. Soon after those calls, the ICU doctor told Amy to get our girls home as soon as possible. My condition was deteriorating. I had aspirated so much that my oxygen levels were dangerously low—doctors were losing hope.

One daughter immediately drove home, while the other caught a flight. Our friend, Patty, met her at the airport and drove her directly to the hospital.

In the middle of the afternoon, a doctor came to meet with Amy in the ICU waiting room. They had done everything they could with medicine, but they were losing me. The only thing left to do was to put me on an extracorporeal membrane oxygenation (ECMO) machine—an extreme form of life support. The machine takes over for the heart and lungs by pumping the patient's blood outside of the body, adding oxygen, removing carbon dioxide, and warming it up, before sending the blood back in, giving the organs a chance to rest and heal. Amy agreed and the staff began the hours-long procedure to put me on the machine.

After 7:00 p.m., I was hooked up to ECMO, and Amy and the girls were finally able to see me. This was tough for them—the girls took it hard. Amy recalled, "It is difficult to explain the level of grief and despair you feel in that moment. When I heard and saw my girls sobbing when they finally got to see their dad...it broke my heart."

The terrible circumstances could have been much worse without the support of friends and family. Numerous close friends and our pastoral staff visited the hospital. Other friends called. Amy called my father, brother, and other relatives.

Even though she was not at the hospital, Sarah was also shaken up. She had just lost her mother two months prior and now her uncle, one of her primary caretakers, was on death's door. Teresa being there to care for her was a godsend.

As the evening went on, a lot of uncertainty remained about whether I would make it through the night. The night nurse told Amy not to leave the hospital, just in case. Our youngest daughter, Caroline, stayed at the hospital with Amy that night. But friends, Kellye, Patty, and Janet thought one of them should also stay, so Kellye stayed. In addition, Mark and Dirk drove my car to the hospital so Amy would have transportation if needed. Teresa sent a night bag with them for Amy and Caroline.

You can not buy friendship like that.

6

VENTURING INTO THE UNKNOWN

The grave concern on the faces of the doctors and nurses was evident, but Amy held onto hope and faith. I made it through the night, but I remained in extreme critical condition. The first couple of days in ICU were filled with anxiety and fear. My condition worsened. Though I was on ECMO, my lung function did not improve and I was now being treated for a severe lung infection. I was on a heavy course of antibiotics and had routine chest X-rays and bronchoscopes to clear my lungs. Two nurses were assigned to me at all times—an ICU nurse and an ECMO nurse.

To check my heart function, a couple transesophageal echocardiograms were performed over the course of a few days. The first test revealed greatly reduced ejection fraction—my left ventricle was barely functional. But, a few days later, another echocardiogram showed improvement.

The reduced heart function caused my body to swell. I accumulated 30 pounds of fluid—further decreasing my lung function. After a few more days on ECMO, my heart improved enough to take me off the heart component; however, my lungs needed the machine support. To help with the switch, fluid needed to be removed. They began giving me Lasix to get the fluid out of my body.

On December 12, five days after I arrived to the hospital, they switched me to the lung only function of the ECMO. This was a big step, but not without complications. Over the next day, they reduced my sedation to get a good neurological check. They had checked this on December 11, but I had very little response. As my sedation was reduced, I also received a number of blood transfusions over a few days. They also discovered that the sodium in my system was very high.

Monday, December 13 was not a good day. With the removal of the sedation, I vomited, my blood pressure dropped, and my fever returned. I also had an ECMO cannulas site that was bleeding at the entry point into my body. The one located on my neck. The staff was not able to stop this bleed entirely and had to continue to supply me with blood.

To top it all off, I was not responsive to the neurological checks. My brain activity was low and there was concern that I had sustained some brain damage. In the next couple days, CT scans of my head were done to identify my lack of response—the results were negative with no explanation. Amy was distraught.

December 14 and December 15 brought more complications. Stool samples determined that I had developed severe internal GI bleeds. An upper and lower GI endoscope was done to locate the bleeding within my stomach and intestines to help resolve the loss of blood.

Though lifesaving, ECMO can lead to clot formation. So, to prevent clots, I was on a heavy dose of the blood thinner heparin. However, if they reduced the dosage, I would be more susceptible to a massive stroke. There is a delicate balance between preventing clots while also preventing internal bleeding. Both can lead to strokes or other complications. I was now bleeding both externally and internally.

Each time the ECMO was turned down to reduce the heparin dosage, my lung function plummeted. All the while, I lay there, eyes sunken, body swollen, little to no brain activity, and completely unaware of the tubes attached all over my body. At one point, the staff switched off the monitor that tracked my brain activity to not discourage Amy even more.

A hospital staff member told Amy that even if I did survive, I would need a heart transplant. One of our pastors, who has been visiting patients in hospitals for 25 years thought I was in the worst condition of anyone he had seen. He began losing hope; he didn't think I would make it.

Amy could barely eat during these days.

Every night on her way home, Amy called my father and brother. Concerned that I would not survive the weekend, she recommended they visit me. Amy was also worried about our girls. As a family, we had already been through so much—the deaths of four close family members in a span of three years, a lot of pain and turmoil in our own immediate family, and now we were navigating the responsibility of raising our niece.

Amy thought if I didn't make it, our girls may never believe in God again.

7

CALL TO ARMS: PRAYER WARRIORS

Amy fueled her faith with a daily routine of prayer and worship. Every day, as she drove to the hospital, she listened to one of my favorite bands, Casting Crowns. Their song, "Praise You In This Storm," became a source of encouragement in a tough, cloudy time. It set her mind and spirit in a good place even in the midst of uncertainty. Once she arrived at the hospital and before she came to my room, she stopped at the chapel adjacent to the ICU to pray for me—to stand in the gap for me. She was confident that if God would just touch me, I would be okay. She was my first prayer warrior.

After only a few days of being in the hospital, Amy decided to have a pastor pray over me every day. She started by asking Pastor Michael to pray and to help her coordinate this prayer effort—he was more than willing. She wanted people to storm the gates of Heaven for my healing. The church responded in force. For 21 days straight, a pastor sat by my bedside and prayed for my healing and for my family. Some of the pastors, I had never met—but they knew it was critical to storm the gates of Heaven on my behalf. In Amy's words, "I will never forget the way they encouraged us and held my daughters' hands and prayed for a miracle for their dad."

Others joined in prayer too. Many close friends prayed. One friend, Jim, prayed on his knees every day and asked God to save me here on earth. Amy started a daily group text with health updates and a reminder to pray. She included a picture of me, pre-cardiac arrest, so that everyone remembered how full of life I had been. Sometimes the image would speak louder than her own words. Word began to spread—again. Group texts multiplied into new group texts as folks passed along the information to others—some who didn't know me personally were praying.

Every night, Amy continued her daily separate phone calls to my dad, brother, and cousin. She called to update them, but their conversations became a source of encouragement for her. She was confident that I would walk out of that hospital one day and she implored everyone to pray and expect that miracle to happen.

On one of the first few nights, Amy showed a nurse a picture of me from a couple weeks before the event. Immediately, the nurse connected with me and saw how full of life I had been. Amy told her that she wanted to bring photos the next day and hang them on the wall so everyone could see the person they were fighting for. That night, before Amy left, the nurse printed color pictures of me from Amy's phone, framed them with construction paper—so they would look nice—and taped them on the walls of my room. It was a huge gesture.

Our neighbor, Joye, had a blanket made with pictures of me that also hung in my hospital room. Folks who came into my room saw these pictures and had an emotional connection to the vibrant, full-of-life guy they were fighting to save.

The outpouring of support for our family was incredible. Aside from the huge blessing of Amy's older sister and Teresa caring for our niece, my family also didn't have to worry about meals or laundry. Our friend, Janet, started and managed a meal train for Amy and our girls. Numerous meal gift cards were given. One friend, Juliet, drove a one-and-a-half-hour round trip several times to bring Amy dinner at the hospital. Liz and Janet also made sure Amy was fed at the hospital and two good friends from church, Kevin and Scott, brought Amy Chick-Fil-A breakfast and left it on our porch.

A few days into my hospital stay, our washing machine broke down. On thing is certain in our household, our washing machine is used every day. It does not get a vacation unless we leave for vacation. But our neighbor, Joye offered to wash our clothes. Amy set it out each morning and Joye returned it at the end of the day. Soon, two of my friends, Steve and Mark, accompanied by a YouTube video, came over and fixed our washing machine.

On one particular day, Janet was on her way to the hospital and listened to the song "Believe For It" by CeCe Winans. This touched her so much that when she got to the hospital, she played it for Amy. This particular day had been especially tough, and together they cried and prayed in the chapel with renewed hope and strength.

Amy literally put one foot in front of the other. However, a movement of people was happening to help and encourage her. People stepped up to be the hands and feet of Jesus. They prayed, visited, helped, fed, and were just present. The movement of people lovingly supported my wife and family. The movement of people stormed the gates of Heaven and implored God to perform a miracle. I now know that the number of people praying for a miracle was in the thousands. People we didn't even know, and still have not met, prayed.

It is hard for me to grasp the gravity of the situation and the enormity of the response. I am humbled when I think about it. At times, it is hard to own and accept that this happened. I do know something happened and it happened because of the faithfulness of many people. Prayer came from people who heard about me from a friend, or from another church, or in a small group, or a social group. Folks prayed who may not have even believed I would survive or who may not have even believed in God.

There is so much to learn from the response of people in those first few weeks. Our family was fortunate to have the support of so many people. But others are in need just like we were—needs are everywhere. What would happen if we harnessed this power from God and used it for others too? How much of a difference could we make in this world if we exhibited the hands and feet of Jesus to those folks as well?

Most of our lives have no margin. We lead complicated, chaotic, busy lives. We do not have the capacity to respond. Or at least we think we don't. Until it happens. When tragedy strikes, it has a way of recalibrating us. We become aware that many of the things we strive for do not matter in the end. These events recenter us to the most important things. What if we didn't wait for a tragedy to occur before we focused on the most important things? What if we recognized the chaos, anxiety, confusion, and striving after the wind for what it is and called it out? What if we live free of these burdens and free to respond to the needs of others? I can think of no greater calling than to love, sacrifice for, and serve others. Isn't that what Jesus modeled?

8

MUDDY WATERS

Prayers were going up. Amy received the following prayer:

"Father God, You have seen this hard time; you knew before it came and you know the way through it. Lord, equip Amy, Caroline, Reagan, Sarah, and their family and friends to walk through what is before them. Only you know Father what will be required-the endurance, the patience, the strength, the wisdom, the courage. Lord, would you meet each and every need ahead of time so that hearts, minds, and bodies would be prepared to tackle the demands of each day. We trust you God, even when things look senseless to us. Lord, help us to keep our gaze fixed on your sufficiency in all things. Protect thoughts from being hijacked by the enemy, fill the Straders with peace from your promises. Lord touch Kevin and heal him supernaturally. Give Amy eyes to see where you are at work today, Lord – may she know your presence is upon her. Have mercy on the Straders. Amen."

On December 16, doctors continued efforts to stop the severe external and internal bleeding and fully remove me from ECMO. Their options were limited though. Heparin caused complications and I needed ECMO to survive. But now was the time to get me off ECMO to see if I could function without it. Before it could be removed completely though, capping trials were conducted to see how my lungs would respond without ECMO. A brief clamp on the machine's gas exchange tested how well my body could function on its own. The first day, I went into respiratory distress within seconds. My breathing was shallow and rapid, so I remained on full function of the machine.

On the second day of trials, the ECMO nurse was even more determined. She spent the morning making sure I was in the best shape possible to take me off ECMO that afternoon. Once again, they removed me from the machine, but this time, I responded better than the day before. With that result, they started to wean me off inhaled nitrous oxide which improves pulmonary blood flow. They also stopped administering heparin with the goal of removing the ECMO cannulas. My fever spiked again. In some ways, it was an "all in" bid to see how I would respond. This method was successful and the order was made to take me off ECMO entirely.

During this time, my brother, sister-in-law, and father visited. At the time, my father was in fragile health, so his good friend Shelton brought him to see me. Amy watched as my father grieved over my condition. He sat on his rollator walker and tried his best to hold onto me. I cannot imagine how he felt after the loss of his wife and his oldest son, and now he was at risk of losing another son.

Even though I was off ECMO, I still had what seemed like a million tubes and wires going in and out of my body, and I was swollen. I did not respond to neurological checks, so doctors ordered an MRI of the brain.

The results showed microbleeds that likely occurred while I

was on ECMO and heparin. A small stroke was also discovered. The findings were deemed insignificant and did not explain my lack of response to neurological checks. On one hand, it was good news that my brain was not damaged, but on the other hand, it had to have been disheartening for my family to not understand why I wouldn't wake up.

All the while, my lung infection and my respiratory status improved and my fever came down. As I've absorbed the hospital notes following my care, it's been overwhelming to read about all the different disciplines of the hospital staff and how they interacted and worked together to save my life. I am greatly appreciative of all they did to get me in a better place without ECMO. We were so blessed to have the healthcare that we did.

While everyone waited for me to wake up, friends and family continued to support Amy and our daughters, who were home on Christmas break. They stepped in and shared household duties to relieve Amy. Sarah went to Columbia for a time to stay with relatives. Folks brought food to the hospital and the house, including a Christmas dinner.

Amy remained a warrior. Though the situation would make you think otherwise, she did not give up on me and she made sure that no one else did either. Her ever presence at the hospital was a reminder to all who cared for me—she would see me walk out of that hospital.

On the morning of December 19, God spoke to Amy. He reassured her by producing a beautiful rainbow for her to see on her drive to the hospital—almost as if he reached out his hand and said, "I got you."

Those moments with God during her own difficult time gave Amy peace and a desire to connect with family members of other ICU patients. "Life in the ICU is tough. There are so many critically ill people. I made friends with the other families in the ICU," Amy said. "A friend lost her husband who was waiting on a heart transplant. That particular morning when I got there, she was standing in the waiting room in a panic. They had called her to come quickly. She needed coffee but was too afraid to leave the waiting room. I went downstairs to get her coffee and came back to sit with her for a few minutes until they came to get her in order to say goodbye to her husband."

She also met an older lady, whose husband who was in heart failure. They prayed for each other, and some nights, ate dinner together. A father was also there to watch over his son who struggled after a heart transplant.

Over the next few days, more work was done on my lungs. I had another procedure to clean them out and a trach was placed to help me breathe more effectively. My respiratory status improved enough to decrease ventilator support. My sedation was off and, in some regards, it was a waiting game. I had periods of rapid, shallow breathing as my lungs adapted to the changes in support.

Then, some hope. I started to sporadically track individuals with my eyes and I moved my arm slightly. These actions were very slight, indicative of being unresponsive or reactionary. So many questions remained as to what my mental state would be when I became fully awake.

During this time, Amy's cousin, Cheryl, and her husband, Kyle visited. At one point, Kyle was alone in the room with me. He talked to me about plans for the annual family Fourth of July fireworks show that he and I had coordinated for the past few years. He was counting on me to get out the hospital and help again. As he talked, I responded. It was just enough for him to feel confident that I could hear and understand him. He reassured Amy that I was going to be okay. That day, Amy wrote in the group text, "Please continue to pray for complete healing. Pray that God puts his healing touch on Kevin today and relieves all pain and performs a Christmas miracle."

Christmas Eve brought more sadness. I was in the ICU and my family had no idea what the future held. It was a tough day for Amy and our girls. To offer their support and bring Amy and our girls some cheer, two friends brought trees and decorations to my ICU room. It was a wonderful gesture.

In the group text, Amy wrote, "It is heartbreaking to sit with my husband in ICU on Christmas Eve. I am ready to see his smile and hear his voice again...Please pray that God heals him soon. We are all weary."

9

AWAKENING

Every morning, Amy woke up at 5:00 a.m. Within a few days of my hospital stay, she had developed an efficient daily cadence. She made sure Sarah was squared away for school and she lined up Sarah's activities for the weekends. She also fed and attended to the three cats and one dog, and accomplished the necessary household chores. Our daughters stepped up to assist as needed. Then, Amy drove to the hospital, parked between 7:00 a.m. and 7:30 a.m., and stopped to pray in the chapel before she arrived to my room in time for the doctors' rounds. Amy had asked to be included in the medical staff meetings that were held outside my door. The doctors agreed to her attendance, but she was only allowed to listen—her questions could be asked at the end.

Every day, a procedure was done to monitor my condition—scans, X-rays, echo, MRI, blood test, or function test. Amy constantly checked the MyChart portal for the results of these procedures and to make sure nothing slipped through the cracks. At one point, she was so hyperfocused on my care that doctors asked if she had a medical background—she does not.

Amy stayed at the hospital throughout the day to keep up with my medical care. When the hospital staff changed shifts around 7:00 p.m., she returned home. On the way, she always made the three calls—my dad, my brother, and my cousin. At home, stood the Christmas tree that I had put up the day before my cardiac arrest. The kids had decorated it in the meantime. Before bed, Amy ensured everything and everyone was cared for before she fell asleep. Typically, with the light on.

At the hospital, I remained unconscious. It was uncertain if I would wake up. If I did, would I neurologically be the same? After a couple of weeks, Amy's positive outlook began to change. Although she was strong and determined, she was weary. Amy could not escape the fact that her husband was in the hospital and would not be home for Christmas. To add to her weariness, because of our history of family losses, one of our girls mentioned to Amy that God does not heal. Amy had no evidence to refute that and she wondered if I would be added to the list.

Although Christmas Eve was a low point for my family, hope arrived on Christmas morning. According to the doctors' notes that day, I was awake and alert.

My family tried to have a normal Christmas morning at the house, wanting to give eight-year-old Sarah a nice Christmas—the first without her mother. After they opened presents and ate breakfast, Amy and our daughters came to the hospital to celebrate with me, while Sarah spent time with her aunt and grandfather. Normally the ICU is limited to two visitors, but the staff made an exception and allowed Amy and our daughters to visit. It was the first day that my girls saw my eyes open. They brought gifts and attempted to show me a video of their Christmas morning. I became sad and cried. They opened a few presents and hung a few more pictures of me and family. The biggest gift was that I was actually responsive. It was slight and weak, but it was a sign of hope and encouragement. I was immediately labeled a Christmas miracle. That day is blurry for me, both in memory and vision, but I do remember a little.

Friends continued to encourage me and my family. Sam and Joan also visited Christmas morning. I remember their faces. I was not able to talk at this point, but I could see and hear them. I responded by blinking my eyes and using facial expressions. They, along with many, many others, had all prayed so hard for my survival, and now they were seeing the fruits of that.

Also on Christmas, a friend on my softball team sent a message to the group text, "I think in many ways Kevin is a Christmas miracle in progress—we just want to have the perfect ending of him again, being able to do things with his family, and friends, and occasionally be able to play a little ball with his softball family. He has also given us some time to be united in our prayer and support for him and his family, and to be sure this Christmas we love and hug and appreciate both our families and the birth of our Savior who makes all of this possible. May we never take any of these blessings for granted—they are a Gift indeed!"

Though many questions remained about my neurological status, hope had been infused into everyone's Christmas. And isn't that what Christmas is all about—hope? Sometimes all you have left is hope and that is what Christmas delivers.

For the next couple of days, I was in and out of consciousness. I became more aware of my surroundings and my condition, and was more responsive to the doctors, nurses, family, and friends. My vision was somewhat blurred, which affected my mental capacity. However, I was aware enough to take in the information that Amy delivered to me from the doctors and nurses, and the friends who visited. But my mind felt slow. I had just woken from a deep sleep, yet I felt ready to drift back to sleep again. All the while, I felt calm.

Every morning a team of doctors and staff assessed my condition and built a plan for the day. A couple days after Christmas, the cardiologist on duty explained to me that I'd had a cardiac arrest, which came as no surprise. I took the news in stride. I believe that's because Amy had already told me that while I was unconscious. She wanted me to know that I was not in the hospital due to a stroke. This was very important to me, as both my brother and mother had suffered debilitating strokes. She didn't want me to worry that I would have the same fate when I awakened.

During the conversation with the cardiologist, he told me that I was not only the sickest person in the hospital, but I was also the sickest person in the entire state of South Carolina. The hospital, MUSC, treats the most severe cases in South Carolina, and apparently, I was it. So at this point I had two labels: A Christmas miracle and the sickest person in all of South Carolina.

10

COMMUNICATING WHEN YOU CAN'T

My surroundings started to become more clear, but I didn't fully understand my physical condition. I did, however, know that I was very weak. In 18 days of unconsciousness, I had lost 34 pounds. I could not verbally communicate—my voice was restricted by a trach and I was very thirsty. Nurses carefully swabbed my mouth with water, as I couldn't swallow. Even if I could, too much water would have caused me to aspirate. A feeding tube provided nutrition for most of my hospital stay. Several of my ribs that were cracked during initial chest compressions had not healed yet. My vision and brain function were not 100 percent. Some of my own family members were unrecognizable in the photos around my room. I didn't even recognize myself in a picture that my daughter took of me in the hospital. *Who was that man with a beard?*

In the few days after Christmas, college football bowl season was in full swing. One nurse, Andy, asked if I was a football fan. Either Amy or myself acknowledged that I was, and he switched the TV to a game. I was in and out of consciousness, but awake enough to watch. But it appeared that the game had changed. To me, the field was half the regular size, with only seven players on each team, and they played with a smaller football than normal. I rationalized this—*maybe they changed the rules due to Covid?* Little did I know, my mind was fuzzy from being unconscious.

An SEC Network commercial with sports reporter Marty Smith ran several times during the games. I became obsessed with the old red Ford pickup in it—I told, or should I say I mouthed, to my youngest daughter, Caroline, that I was going to buy it one day.

I could not talk, and although I tried to mouth words to everyone, I became frustrated with that method. Caroline and Amy had become better at figuring out what I was saying, but it was a laborious method of communication. To help, my family bought me a small dry erase board. However, when they gave me the board and a marker, my hands shook vigorously. I was too weak to hold the marker. I tried to write a word, but could hardly get a letter down. Frustration began to build.

To add to it, I had to use a bedpan to use the bathroom. Nurses are trained to help patients with this experience—but this patient was humiliated. It's one of the last things you want done for you. So, with my room's bathroom toilet in sight, I was determined to use it rather than a bedpan. However, as mentioned, I had no idea of my physical condition. I had no idea how many tubes and wires prevented me from getting out of the bed. But these details did not deter me from trying. What followed is now a humorous chain of events. I waited until no one was looking and then slowly slid my left leg off the bed in the direction of the toilet. But my daughter, wife, or a nurse would notice that my leg had moved off the bed and one of them would quickly place it back on the bed. My family would then admonish me. I attempted several times, with no clue that I physically could not get off the bed. Not only did I have tubes and wires connected to me, but my ribs were broken, which kept me from sitting up. At one point, I became so frustrated that my efforts were being squashed, I threw a pillow at my daughter—my arms worked. Looking back, this is all very funny. But at the time, it was leading me to a low point.

I was stuck in bed. From there, I noticed a bottle on a shelf. I recognized it as a bottle of water and I was so thirsty. Just like my desire to use the toilet, I focused on how I could get to this bottle. But again, I had no idea what kind of shape I was in or that, even if I could reach the "water," I couldn't swallow. First, I had a trach inserted, and second, I learned later, that my ability to swallow was severely impacted, almost all of it would go into my lungs. Though determined, my body and other restrictions made it impossible for me to obtain my objective. This added to my frustration, driving me to an even lower point. Later, I learned that the bottle was not even water, but a different substance that would have made me sick.

Days passed. I knew the season, but I had no concept of the day of the week. At night, I stared at the nurses who sat at the desk outside my room. The world seemed to continue on. But I had no idea what it was like past those opaque doors. All I knew was that someone was there if I needed help. At the same time, I felt lonely. Without verbal communication, I just stared and wondered if I would get better.

I was also very hot—I always seemed to be sweating. I was able to communicate this and the nurses brought me a fan. That was a big help. Normally I am cold natured—a product of living in the South and getting older. Now, my body reacted differently.

I had never desired to drink water as much as I did then. Nurses continued to douse a swab in water and hand it to me to suck up as much water as I possibly could. At the time, this had to be a part of Heaven. At one point, one of my nurses mentioned swapping the water for ginger ale. Amy or I must have affirmed this idea, as they had extreme compassion for me. Just like the water, they used a swab to give me a little ginger ale. It had to have been the best thing I ever had in my life—I became obsessed with ginger ale. It's hard to describe what this little gesture did for my soul, but I can tell you I will never forget it.

I eventually graduated to ice chips. The nurse brought a cup of ice and gave me one or two pieces. The staff remained careful not to give me too much—a balancing act of substance to chew on, but not too much to aspirate on. At this time, anything I swallowed would almost assuredly end up in my lungs. So they had to be conservative and only give me something that would mostly absorb in my mouth. It took almost my entire hospital stay to learn how to swallow again. However, just like the ginger ale, ice chips were a treat. Eventually, I was able to hold a cup of ice on my own and chew on a few pieces.

Aside from swallowing, I also noticed that my hearing was not right. I had worn hearing aids for several years, but when I put them in now, I couldn't hear properly out of my right ear. I thought it was the hearing aid, so Amy asked our neighbor to have them looked at. The report came back that there was no issue with the hearing aids. I was not convinced. Several days went by and I still had an issue with my right ear. I asked for the hearing aids to be looked at again—the same report came back. So, I just dealt with the inconvenience. At the time, I did not understand the severity of my hearing loss, but other issues overshadowed this one, so we would deal with my hearing later.

These early days felt like being awakened from a deep sleep and being unsure of where you are. Your mind is fuzzy as you try to process what is going on. You know you're safe, but at the same time, you don't understand how you got to this place. I couldn't get a handle on my condition or what landed me in the hospital. Ultimately, it led me to a place of discouragement and helplessness.

However, in the background, people continued to pray. One prayer sent to Amy read:

"I know the ups and downs are literally tearing you down. You are strong and God is by your side. Your family is standing in the gap with you. 'God is within her, She will not fall'" Psalms 46:5 (NIV).

Another one read:

"I love that we are now praying for complete healing! A week ago we were praying for him to wake up! I'm claiming a Christmas miracle."

11

DISCOURAGEMENT: NEVER GETTING OUT OF THE BED

Three days after I woke up, I was introduced to two individuals who would become some of my best friends at the hospital. But they did not start that way.

Josie and Kara, my occupational and physical therapists, returned to work after the Christmas holiday with the responsibility of getting me out of bed. They arrived to my room as their energetic and optimistic selves, determined to accomplish this task—that week. I had no idea what I was in for.

By now, my determination to get out of bed to use the toilet had sailed down the river. I was quite content watching college football on TV. The humbling process of using a bedpan was more desirable than attempting to sit up—let alone stand. Each time I needed to use the bedpan, a nurse lined it with pads, rotated me on my side and positioned the bedpan for use. Then, the nurse cleaned me up and rotated me back in bed. What a gracious, compassionate, and selfless exercise nurses go through.

At this point, I had laid in bed for three weeks. I only moved when someone rotated me side to side. However, Josie and

Kara intended to change that. Their first day working with me, they had one goal—get me to stand.

First, they encouraged me to sit up and then rotate my legs off the bed. Just sitting up seemed impossible. Up to this point, I had only been able to get myself in a slumped, uncomfortable position. I had lost 34 pounds and was very weak, so I couldn't readjust myself in the bed. Two nurses had to move me for X-rays, or reset my position in the bed using a bed sheet.

But Josie and Kara were determined. They raised the bed and tried to help me sit up. Immediately, I realized how bad of shape I was in. Within seconds, my head spun, and I swayed and swayed and was very dizzy. My ribs hurt and I had no core strength, I was miserable. I felt sick to my stomach and my body ached. The two ladies held me up and encouraged me. All I wanted to do was lie back in bed. Soon, Kara and Josie conceded and let me rotate back into bed. That was the end of my first OT and PT session. I didn't know what to think of that event, or of those two ladies.

The next day, they returned—energetic and optimistic. I, on the other hand, wasn't sure I was glad to see them. But, Josie and Kara repeated the process anyway. They helped me sit up and rotate, and then they encouraged me to put my feet on the floor. I trembled and swayed, dizzy and hurting. I was anxious and nervous. They were relentless. I, however, felt defeated. I hadn't completely grasped how bad of shape I was in until those two days. I was weak and broken—my body didn't feel like my own. I had always been fairly active, and now, I couldn't even hold myself in a seated position. Josie and Kara ended the session and visited two more times that week. I made some progress, but I still couldn't get out of the bed to stand.

To say I was discouraged is an understatement. Later, I learned that Josie and Kara were somewhat surprised and also concerned about my ability to recover. But that didn't stop them from trying a new technique after the New Year's weekend.

As my daughters prepared to return to college that week, they visited me several times, and our family visits were wonderful. I had improved enough to sit up in bed, with help from the mechanical hospital bed which could transition into a chair at the press of a few buttons. My lungs were now strong enough to wear a trach collar for a couple hours each day, allowing me to speak more easily. The respiratory therapist would swap out my trach for the collar and monitor my oxygen saturation to ensure I was breathing well. For the first time, I could carry on conversations with my family which made our visits really special.

I was able to catch up with my kids' lives. In another week they would head back to college, so it was great that I was able to talk to them. Caroline made a decision to transfer to another college, a decision we talked about before my cardiac arrest, but I hadn't heard of her final decision. I was hopeful she would make the change and happy to hear this news.

Caroline also told me about her last week of exams that had started when I had my cardiac arrest. Not a good time for an emergency. But her professors were gracious and flexible, and she was allowed to take the exams from home. She updated me on the move out of her dorm. Her good friend, and her friend's father helped her move out and brought everything to our home. It was a tremendous gesture and another example of how people rallied around Amy and the kids to help in this difficult time. Caroline would transfer to a college within minutes of my brother Stephen's home in Nashville. Stephen visited me while I was unconscious and returned to his home with a load of Caroline's belongings. I was a little sad that I would not have the opportunity to move her into her new place, as was normally my duty. But I am so grateful to friends and my brother who filled that gap for me.

Reagan would return to her school for her final semester. She would graduate the following spring of 2022. Even though she was returning to her same dorm, I would also miss my usual privilege of moving her back in for the semester.

The week ended up being pretty emotional. It was time to say goodbye to both of my daughters. They had spent as much time as they could with me, and I'm sure it was difficult for them to leave me in this condition.

Before Caroline left, she surprised me with a gift. I craved ginger ale, and now, I had graduated to ice chips. Caroline purchased a couple ice chip trays, made ginger ale ice chips, and snuck them in for me. Let me tell you, that was a fantastic surprise!

Some of the hospital staff and our friends had left for the New Year's holiday weekend and I had a lot of time to reflect on my situation. It was not good. I was discouraged. The full weight of my condition was upon me. One blow after another seemed to bear down on me.

In addition to the previously mentioned ailments, a few others added to my weakness. My left leg was numb and I had a knot around my knee. I learned that this was due to being on ECMO. Doctors connected me to the machine using a blood vessel in that leg, which led to complications and caused me discomfort.

On top of that, Amy told me that I had incurred a mini-stroke. The doctors weren't concerned about it, neither was the neurosurgeon my daughter and I saw in 2014, who reviewed my MRI. But it was one more thing on the pile of things that I had to deal with. My right shoulder also ached. Months later, I learned that I had two torn tendons, a frayed bicep tendon, and an inflamed bursa—likely from years of playing softball and the repositioning of my body while I was unconscious. If that wasn't enough, weeks of lying in bed caused me to develop two bedsores on the back of my head. The wound care team visited me on a consistent basis to prevent infection.

In addition, my trach was uncomfortable. It required frequent suction to remove phlegm buildup near its opening and it needed to be managed regularly.

Routine chest X-rays helped doctors monitor the condition of my lungs and fractured ribs. To combat the lung infection, an infectious disease physician was assigned to prescribe me antibiotics.

Aside from medical complications, after a few weeks, my body was in need of some serious personal hygiene. I had not bathed, I had extremely dry skin, my beard and nails had grown long, my hair was matted, and my teeth needed brushed—despite a feeding tube for most of my stay. Amy wore many hats while I was in the hospital and that included her attention to these items. She either did them herself or ensured someone did them for me. I am overwhelmed when I think about all she managed and that she kept herself together in the process.

In the hospital, I had a lot of time to reflect on all that had happened, but I could not remember the days leading up to my cardiac arrest. I had short-term memory loss. I've been told that the night before I collapsed, I had taken our niece to swim practice and put up our Christmas tree. Two days prior, we had lunch with Amy's cousin and her family in Columbia, South Carolina. While there, we also spent time with our daughter, who attended school there. I could not remember that. I also could not remember that we had dinner with friends just four days before my event. I vaguely remember Thanksgiving that year. Some of these memories have returned, but many have never fully been regained.

An uptick in Covid cases caused the hospital to reinstitute Covid restrictions. I would no longer see regular visitors. Alone in my room—more nights of lying in bed, staring at the nurse's station outside my door. *Would I ever get out of this bed on my own and leave this room?*

12

DECISION: FIGHTING GRAVITY

Over New Year's weekend, it hit me. *A lot of people are counting on me to get out of this bed.* Word about my hospitalization spread throughout our church, other churches, social media, and text messages. The number of people praying for me to survive and recover was in the thousands.

Amy wrote in the group text to everyone: "There have been numerous staff that have come to visit him. One respiratory therapist told me yesterday with tears in her eyes that she was here the day they brought him into the ICU. They fought hard to save him, but were not hopeful he would make it. He is my Christmas miracle! Keep praying!!!"

I received numerous visits from friends, family, church members, and even members of other churches. Amy gave me a glimpse of the number of people praying, but I didn't comprehend how many until months after leaving the hospital. I also learned about the role our neighbors, Joye and Jack played to save my life. Through one of our friends, Joan, I heard how strong Amy had been through everything. Amy was labeled a warrior by a number of people in our church.

I made a decision. It was time—I was going to get out of bed. That weekend, I asked Amy when Kara and Josie were returning to continue our therapy sessions. Too many people were invested in my recovery and I wasn't going to let them down.

Just like clockwork, Kara and Josie showed up after the weekend. I was ready. However, being reintroduced to gravity made for an interesting day. This time, they brought a new contraption that I hadn't seen before—a cardiac walker. It looked straight out of Star Wars, but it quickly became my new best friend. Its design allowed me to hold myself upright and it provided a place to sit if I became tired.

I was just as weak as before, but I was undeterred. I required Kara and Josie's assistance to sit up and rotate my body to the edge of the bed. I had made up my mind, I was getting out of that bed and I would listen to their instructions to accomplish my goal.

With their help, I accomplished the first task; I sat up on the side of the bed. Now, stand up. Ignoring gravity for four weeks made it fight me—hard. I pushed up against gravity and my body trembled. I could not believe how hard it was just to stand. It's something you never think about, you just do. For over 50 years, I stood up without a thought, but that day it was the only thought I had. My legs trembled, my body ached, and I was light headed and dizzy. But I had made a commitment to myself, I was not going to quit this time. I pushed on. I grabbed the arms of the cardiac walker, and with as much strength as I could, I began to pull myself up. Over four years later, I vividly remember that moment. On January 3, even with all the adversity and setbacks, I grasped the walker and stood up.

The room lit up. Josie, Kara, Amy, and the nurses were elated. What seemed impossible the week prior—and an eternity from December 7—was now a reality. I was out of the bed. I was proud of myself. As a bonus, now that I was upright,

Kara and Josie asked me to accomplish another task: take a step. With their help, guidance, and protection, I slid one foot forward. It too was weird. Then, I slid the other foot forward. I stood there and looked at Kara and Josie.

That was it. We were done for the day. Kara and Josie said I had accomplished that day's therapy session and I would have to wait until the next day. With their help, I sat back down on the bed and returned to my normal lying down position. But I was ready for more.

It is hard to describe how thankful I am for those women and for everyone who cared for me in the hospital. Because of that, I tried to get to know each of my caretakers—nurses, doctors, technicians, Kara, and Josie. As they returned each week, I asked them questions about their lives, like, where they were from and about their families. It was important to me to really know them.

My two new best friends, Kara and Josie, arrived the next day and I was ready. They showed up with my other new best friend, the cardiac walker. I had seen that "Star Wars" contraption before, so I wasn't intimidated this time. I knew it could help me. Once again, they helped me sit and rotate out of bed. Gravity fought me again. They positioned the walker in front of me and I grasped the handles. I began the arduous process of pushing and pulling myself to a standing position. This time though, I knew I could overcome, and I pushed forward.

Mission accomplished! Once I stood, Kara and Josie gave another instruction: walk. With a chair in the room as my destination, I wondered how I would make the eight-foot walk to reach it. Again, what should be a thoughtless activity, now consumed all my thoughts. *How do I take a step?* Kara and Josie coached me, my legs weak and trembling, I took a step—more like a slide of my foot. And then another step. Then another. Now I was walking toward it. I got to the chair and Kara and Josie helped me turn around and sit down in it. That was the end of my therapy session. That day, I got out of bed and walked.

I sat in the chair for a while and thought a lot about what had just happened. A few days earlier, I wondered if I would ever get out of the bed. Now, I sat in a chair that I had walked to with the help of two fantastic ladies and a cardiac walker.

It makes you wonder how close you are to a breakthrough. It may come through a simple decision and the help of other people to make it happen.

13

MOVING FORWARD IN THE FACE OF ADVERSITY

Josie and Kara walked through the sliding doors of my room. I was ready. Amy had arrived before them to prepare me for another therapy session. With their help, I rotated in bed and sat up. Cardiac walker in front of me, I grasped the handles, fought gravity, and stood. Then the news of a new goal—walk out of the room and down the hall. I had not been out of my room since I arrived at the hospital. I had only caught small glimpses from my bed when the door was open. So, without further ado, we began. One step in front of the other.

The hospital staff was right outside my room, as they were every morning to discuss my case. Doctors, residents, physician assistants, and nurses were gathered to review my progress and make a plan for the day. With Kara and Josie's guidance, I walked through the doors of my room, turned left, and walked past the staff toward the big windows at the end of the hall. According to Amy, the entire staff stopped their conversation and watched me. They were amazed and could not believe what they were seeing. In some ways, they were witnessing something they never thought possible. They saw a man who had lain in bed for four weeks, who had knocked on death's door many times. A man who had been unconscious for 18 days and on life support for 11 of them. A man who had lost 34 pounds and was labeled the sickest person in South Carolina. That same man just walked past them and down the hall.

I got to the end of the hallway and stopped. The great thing about the cardiac walker is the built-in chair. I sat down in front of the windows and peered out onto the Charleston skyline—a fantastic sight. It was a sunny day. Imagine being cooped up in your home all winter and then suddenly a warm spell breaks through the cold, inviting you outside with the promise of spring. That's how I felt. *Maybe I would finally be able to leave one day and be outside again, with the sun shining on me.*

I sat there for a few moments and took it all in. However, it was time to get back to work. I stood up, rotated the walker 180 degrees, and started toward my room. It was then that I noticed the staff outside my room. It was like a crowd at the marathon finish line waiting to cheer on the runners. Their eyes were on me. I gave them a nod and a wink, as if to say, "I got this." I walked past them, into my room, and back to my bed. Though it was exciting, I was spent. That day, Wednesday, January 5, was another day of adventure, and one that would be remembered for a long time.

Although a walk down the hall was a big accomplishment, I had a long way to go. I had only been awake for one and a half weeks. My lungs were in bad shape, so a trach assisted with breathing and I was only allowed to crunch on ice chips. Questions remained regarding my ability to swallow.

That day, I received a visit from the speech therapist who conducted a barium swallow test to determine if I could properly swallow liquids and solids. I was in for a surprise. The test uses an active X-ray machine to monitor the flow of various liquids and solids as they make their way down the esophagus and into the stomach. The test begins with the patient trying to swallow liquids of varying consistencies to determine if an individual can properly swallow without any liquid entering the lungs, known as aspirating. That day, it didn't take long to determine that I could not swallow, not even the easiest liquid. It was another reminder that I had a number of issues to deal with. I was disappointed, but was not devastated. I had hoped for a better result, but at the time, I didn't think it was serious. However, learning to swallow would become the biggest obstacle before I could be discharged from the hospital.

My hearing also continued to be problematic, particularly my right ear. It was the same issue I noticed shortly after I woke up. My hearing aids were checked again a couple of times, but I still did not have full hearing in my right ear. Doctors discussed possibilities, but at the time, it was not a high priority. I was worried, but assumed it would be rectified.

For the most part, I have nothing but great things to say about the MUSC staff for their care and support as I healed from these life-altering conditions. However, three events occurred during my stay that were not pleasurable and could have been handled better. I almost hate writing about them, as I carry a tremendous amount of gratitude regarding the stay. But, sometimes things do happen, and I want to highlight the importance of having a family member, friend, or advocate with you when you're in the hospital.

A few days after I regained consciousness, I knew I was in pretty bad shape. I was weak, my fractured ribs were healing, and I couldn't speak or swallow. I was in no shape to get out of bed, not in my own power.

But one night, one of my nurses obviously didn't get the message that I couldn't leave the bed on my own. The nurse arrived to my room with every intention of having me get out of bed and walk to the chair. With a trach in, I could not talk, and without the help of a trained PT and OT, I had not stood up on my own. That didn't matter—she was determined.

Sometime between 4:00 a.m. and 5:00 a.m., the nurse tried to get me to sit up. I could not do it. I knew what shape I was in. At this point, I hadn't even stood yet without Kara and Josie's help. To the best of my ability, I tried to let the nurse know that I could not do what she wanted. I shook my head vigorously. She was persistent. She berated me and told me I had to get out of bed. Even in my state, I knew this was the job of PT. She was not the right person. Finally, she left me alone. I dodged a bullet, or so I thought, and I didn't think anything else of it.

Soon, she returned with a nurse's aide who had cared for me on previous nights. He knew my condition, but I could see that he was conflicted against the nurse's will. This time, she would not take no for an answer and used the gurney and hoist to move me to the chair. Once again, I fought her using facial expressions and shaking my head, but I was powerless. With the aide's help, she got me in the gurney and hoisted me into the chair. She was proud of herself. I was traumatized.

Now that I was in the chair, they left the room and were out of sight. I sat alone again in the early morning hours, but at least the chaos left my room...for a minute. Almost immediately, the trach tube popped off my neck. This hadn't happened before and I was freaked out. I grabbed the tube, but I couldn't see where to reattach it. I hadn't been without the trach tube and supplemental oxygen, so I had no idea what would happen. But I knew I had an emergency. It was a moment of panic. Without thinking to use the call button, I felt around the trach opening on my neck and reattached the tube. It popped off again. Finally, I secured it and calmed myself down. Overall, I handled it well.

If I put myself in the nurse's shoes, I can understand her motivation to get me out of bed. To see a patient lie in bed day after day can be deflating. Nurses are there to care for you, but they also want you to improve. However, this early in my recovery, she went overboard on her responsibility and put her own motivations in front of my situation. It made for a stressful and unnecessary experience, especially on night shift where there is less oversight.

Later that morning, my hero, Amy, showed up. I explained to her what happened by mouthing the words and motioning with my hands. Immediately, she contacted the charge nurse and had a conversation. I never had that particular nurse again.

On a separate night shift, a few days after awakening, I was introduced to a machine that would assist with my breathing so I could be weaned off the trach. But this imposed the second stressful situation. The respiratory therapist who switched me to the machine was nice, but I became skeptical of the procedure being part of the overall plan. To make matters more difficult, I couldn't talk to express my concern. Amy had to go home, but fortunately, my daughter Caroline stayed with me.

Once the machine was fitted on me, I was instructed to sleep with the contraption powered on. The respiratory therapist flipped the switch. Immediately, I knew this would be trouble. Air was blowing into my lungs, and up and around my face and neck. It was not a pleasant experience. It was noisy and uncomfortable, and though this may not have been the case, I felt like I was suffocating. *There's no way I'm going to survive this, let alone get any rest.*

My daughter saw me struggle and she too became stressed. She searched for a nurse and the respiratory therapist who returned to inspect the setup and reassured us that everything would be okay. I, on the other hand, wanted this thing gone. That was not going to happen. My daughter tried her best, but eventually called Amy. Within an hour, Amy returned to the hospital to relieve Caroline. My wife, who had been at the hospital every day for 12 hours straight, nonstop since I entered the hospital, returned at midnight to spend the night with me.

Amy jumped into action and talked to my nurse—it was heated. Amy was my advocate and the nurse was following instructions for the patient. Fortunately, a decision was made to remove the contraption for that evening. Constant oxygen monitoring tested how my lungs functioned without the machine and the staff would be alarmed if I ran into trouble. Amy would also hear alarms if they were to go off that night. Once the machine was removed, it was like a blanket of stress was removed too. I was able to rest without the support, which ended up being a blessing in disguise. My lungs held up with no issues and I could transition into the next steps of being weaned off the trach.

One huge benefit from this experience was that the staff was ready to test a trach collar, a good test to check my lung progress. I never got to see what it looked like on me though. But it allowed me to do two things: breath on my own without support, and this is a biggie...I could now communicate verbally with my friends and family for the first time since I came to the hospital.

As time went on, I tested well on the trach collar. So the next step was to do a "quick swap" of trachs—a trach reduction, which led to the third event that could have been handled better. The first reduction was one of the most painful experiences I've ever had. I've had broken bones, torn ligaments, cuts, been hit with baseballs, you name it. Nothing touched the pain I experienced with this procedure.

Two doctors, I believe both residents at the time, did the swap. I was laid back in bed and held down. To this day, I have no idea of the steps involved. All I know is something was pulled out and something was put in. When the procedure began, I nearly came off the bed. My vision became blurred. I coughed and wretched. It was not a good experience. Later, while in the step-down unit, I had another trach reduction. That one was seamless. I still wonder what happened this first time to make it so painful.

Then, after 30 days in the ICU, came news of progress. I was being moved to the step-down unit. I had improved, but I still had a number of issues. Like being on a trach, not swallowing properly, just starting to walk, using a bedpan, and I had hearing issues, among other hurdles. I guess my walk down the hallway was impressive enough to let me move on. This was a big day—I know it was for Amy. She had visited me in that same room for a month, and for most of it, I was unconscious.

Before I could leave the ICU, I needed to have a PICC line inserted. Since I could not swallow and needed antibiotics to clear my lungs, the medicine would be administered intravenously. My room was cleared of everyone and sanitized for a minor surgery procedure. My arm was also sanitized, as this line had direct access to my heart. From my bed, three medical staff members placed the IV line in my upper arm, straight toward my heart. An ultrasound machine was used to accurately place the line. In just under an hour they had me fixed up. This was a lot better than the trach reduction. I now had the green light to move to the step-down unit.

That day, a crew showed up to move me out of my room. I was able to stand on my own and move to a wheelchair. As I was wheeled out of my room, we took a right-hand turn and I took it all in. Up until then, I had only seen a small portion of the ICU outside my room. We passed nursing stations and the main station in the middle. Numerous nurses wished me well—some I recognized. I'm sure this was big for them too. These nurses see and experience so much and a great deal is not pleasurable. So, to see someone get well enough to leave has to be gratifying for them.

In a way, I hated to leave. I had grown close to the ICU staff and became comfortable with the routine. I was excited to have made progress, but moving to another floor brought anxiety about my care. But once I arrived in my new room and met my new caretakers, whatever anxiety I had was gone.

All the while, prayers and support continued. A prayer sent to Amy that day read,

"Father God, We ask that you continue the healing. We thank you for the ways you have used medicine and a wise medical team to save and strengthen Kevin. God, we ask that you would continue to give decisive clarity, wisdom, and precision to the team of doctors and nurses in charge of his care. We ask that you would just baffle them with Kevin's progress toward complete recovery of strength, ability, and wellness. God, would you grant Amy, Reagan, Caroline, and Sarah the endurance to walk this difficult journey. As they return to school and the rhythms of daily responsibilities, would you surround them with your love and care–through your Holy presence and through a community that supports them well. Thank you Lord! In Jesus' name, Amen."

14

GETTING MY MIND RIGHT

I woke up around 7:00 a.m. each morning. The first morning in step-down, I met my first resident doctor for that unit. She was blown away by how healthy I looked. She had read my medical records from my time in ICU and her mental picture of my condition did not match the alert and energetic man in front of her. She was assigned to me that first week and returned every morning around 7:00 a.m.—she became another buddy.

The move to step down was actually a step up in my recovery. I still faced a number of issues, but we had an organized plan to tackle them. Just like in ICU, a team of doctors met outside my room each morning to discuss my case and then they delivered the daily plan to Amy and me. It was vital to clear the remaining hurdles so I could leave the hospital. We worked together to overcome hearing loss, swallowing, using the bedpan, the trach, learning to walk, among many others.

Considering everything I had been through, I thought I looked pretty good—until I saw myself in a mirror. Amy and I established a daily routine. She usually arrived around 7:30 a.m. to help me get ready for the day. I was awake enough to chat before she gave me a bath with hygienic wipes and "washed" my hair with dry shampoo. By then, I was able to brush my own teeth, so I would knock that out then, too.

Once cleaned up, Amy and I wrote questions for the doctors, like, why did I go into cardiac arrest? When they arrived later, we collaborated and set goals for the day. But before that meeting, a fantastic event occurred.

I wanted to be cleaned up and ready by 9:00 a.m. everyday. That's when Kara and Josie arrived and I got to walk again. Unhooked from the monitors and equipped with supplemental oxygen and local monitors, Kara and Josie helped me stand. I grabbed hold of my friend, the cardiac walker, and took off.

For a couple of days, the objective was to walk down the hallway and back. The walk was a little further than the one I took in ICU. Though I enjoyed the walk down and back, it was exhausting. I was weak, and you do not realize how hard gravity works against you after you've ignored it for a month.

After the walk, Kara situated me into the chair in my room. It was great to get out of bed and sit in a chair for a change. However, I had lost so much weight that I couldn't get comfortable. I was skin and bones, with no cushion on my backside anymore. I wanted to sit in the chair, but it was a chore. We tried propping me up with pillows, but it didn't work. So Amy, once again took action, and with the help of Amazon Prime, a donut pillow and memory-foam pillows arrived. This was a huge help and made it possible for me to sit in the chair for several hours.

That day, Amy's text to everyone read: "As I sit and talk with my husband today, I am amazed and thankful that God performed a miracle to save him. December 7 is a day that will always be etched in my memory, but so incredibly blessed that there will be more memories with Kevin. He is an incredible man who completes me and makes me a better person. He continues to improve. The lung CT shows improvement in his lungs. The new cardiologist is phenomenal and is really trying to get Kevin on the right medicine and make sure that everything possible is done to prevent another heart attack. Kevin was able to walk down the hall with a stand-up walker today. He is so motivated to get stronger quickly. He is a fighter! I cannot thank everyone enough for all the help during this difficult time. You guys have literally been the hands and feet of Jesus for our family! Keep praying for healing and endurance!"

Within a couple of nights in step down, one of the night nurses encouraged me to graduate from the bedpan and use the bedside toilet. I still needed assistance, but this was another big step. I have never been more humbled than when a nurse had to help me use a bedpan.

After four weeks of being cooped up in the controlled hospital environment, I finally got a sense of the cold, fresh air outside—a reminder that it was winter beyond those doors. I had missed all of the Christmas and New Year's activities. As nice as it was to feel the fresh air, the adventure outdoors was not under the best terms, or a simple task. An Ear, Nose, and Throat (ENT) resident reviewed my current antibiotic regimen for my severe lung infection to determine whether it might be contributing to my hearing loss. I was also prescribed steroids to see if it would improve my hearing. To determine the severity, I was sent for testing in a different part of the hospital, not accessible by wheelchair. A transport team moved me to a stretcher, wheeled me outside, and loaded me into the back of an ambulance.

This ambulance ride was drastically different than my urgent ride on December 7. Now I was keenly aware of my surroundings. Prior to my cardiac arrest, I had never been in an ambulance and I wasn't awake to remember it. But on this short ride to the Children's Hospital, the only testing booth available, I observed everything. I noticed where the paramedic sat and I observed the equipment that hung from the sides of the vehicle. It was surreal. I could only imagine what December 7 was like.

Once in the hearing test booth, two audiologists fitted me with testing equipment. I was familiar with these tests, having had them in years past. That day's test confirmed that I had significant hearing loss in my right ear and slight hearing loss in my left. Questions remained as to how this happened and whether or not it could be reversed. To find out, I needed an MRI to get a view of the area around my ears. Since it was not urgent, I waited for a break in the schedule. Lucky for me, they had an opening in the middle of the night! The night shift gave me a heads up that it might happen then, but it still came as a surprise when the crew showed up around midnight to wheel me down for a test. The images revealed bone loss in my skull above my inner ear with no definitive evidence of the cause. It could have always existed, but it also could have also been a result of being on ECMO.

Later, after leaving the hospital, an otologist explained that the most likely scenario is that the nerves in my ear were damaged due to the lack of blood flow during cardiac arrest. As I write, my hearing has not been restored and we are still seeking options to bring it back.

Three bigger issues remained: Why did my heart go into ventricular fibrillation (VFib), and how do we address that? How does my lung damage heal so I can get off the trach? And how can I swallow again? A fourth issue was also present, damage to my right shoulder, but it wouldn't be rectified until a year later.

With so many obstacles in the way, my days in step down were filled with tests, exercises, and activities that were meant to help me regain strength and health. I was so focused on recovery that I rarely watched TV, except to try to catch some of the College Football National Championship game. My time in step down was, for the most part, all business. I wanted to get better and I wanted to go home.

My heart was still a concern. Doctors didn't find any blockages or plaque buildup when I arrived at the hospital on December 7, so they continued to determine if there was any damage to my heart or other abnormalities. I was wheeled to the radiology department for an MRI; however, one big issue stood in the way—I couldn't lie flat. My throat was irritated from the trach reduction a few days earlier, and quite a bit of phlegm had to be suctioned out. I coughed a lot, and lying flat made it worse. This was problematic because you must be completely still in the MRI machine. This one would last over an hour. The radiology technician was extremely patient, she waited for me to work through the coughing and gain control. Once I got past that point, I was positioned on my back and slid into the narrow tube for the MRI.

An MRI is quite an experience, it's not for the claustrophobic. The machine is loud, it can sound like a broken piece of machinery at times. The technicians give you ear plugs and, oftentimes, headphones to listen to music as a distraction and to soothe you. For me, I usually need more than ear plugs and music. This time, I tried to remember all the camping trips that my family ever took, there must have been over 40 trips. For several years our family camped in either a pop-up tent camper or a travel trailer. They were some of our best vacations. As I lay there, I recalled memories from the locations and our experiences. I remembered the many trips to Hunting Island near Beaufort, South Carolina and swinging in a hammock by Lake Jocassee in upstate South Carolina. I remembered trips with friends to the Outer Banks of North Carolina and Deep

Creek near Bryson City, North Carolina. Between focusing on holding back coughs and thinking of the great times our family had, I made it through the scan.

For the most part, my heart looked normal. The cardiologist determined that a section of my heart was scarred, typical with a heart attack. Heart attacks are usually caused by a blockage, but no evidence of a blockage existed. My heart looked healthy and normal. My cardiologist, one of the most experienced cardiologists at the hospital, thinks my cardiac arrest was a one-off event and would probably never happen again. Still today, it's a mystery as to why it happened. The bigger question is, how do we prevent it from occurring again?

I began my own search for answers, mainly online, but I was also presented with an option that would help if another VFib episode ever occurred again—an implantable cardio-verter-defibrillator (ICD). It's designed to monitor the heart's activity and if I were to go into VFib again, the device would shock my heart back into rhythm. Without answers to the future of my heart's function, Amy and I consulted with several specialists, like electro physiologists who place medical devices in the body to assist with managing certain heart arrhythmias. In my case, the use of a defibrillator on board would be a so-called first responder if my heart ever raced to the point of cardiac arrest.

Just like every day, Amy and I put together a list of questions for the different doctors that would visit the next day. Over several meetings, we quizzed physicians about the use of the device, purpose of it, justification for having it, and the downsides of living with it. I was not crazy about having a medical device inside my chest, but eventually, I came around to understanding the justification and conceded to the placement. But I was in no physical condition to have that done yet. I was still learning to walk and my lung infection needed to heal.

In the meantime, I would not be discharged without temporary protection—a life vest. The external device was cumbersome, but, if needed, the strapped-on defibrillator around my chest could restart my heart until I received the ICD implant six weeks after returning home.

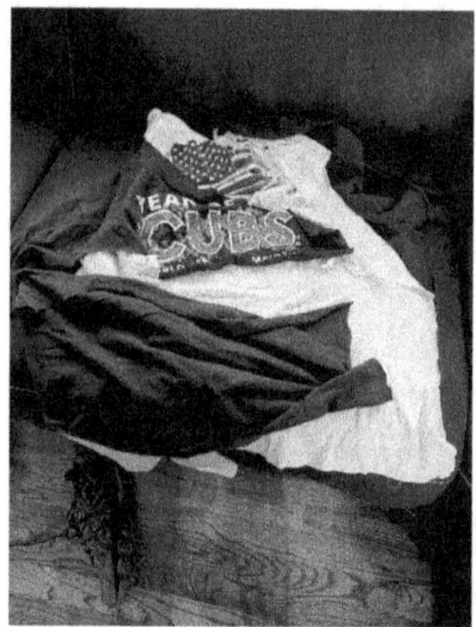

Chaos: On December 7, paramedics had to cut
away my shirt to perform CPR and administer
defibrillator shocks. Later, my brother gifted me a
new Cubs shirt as a replacement.

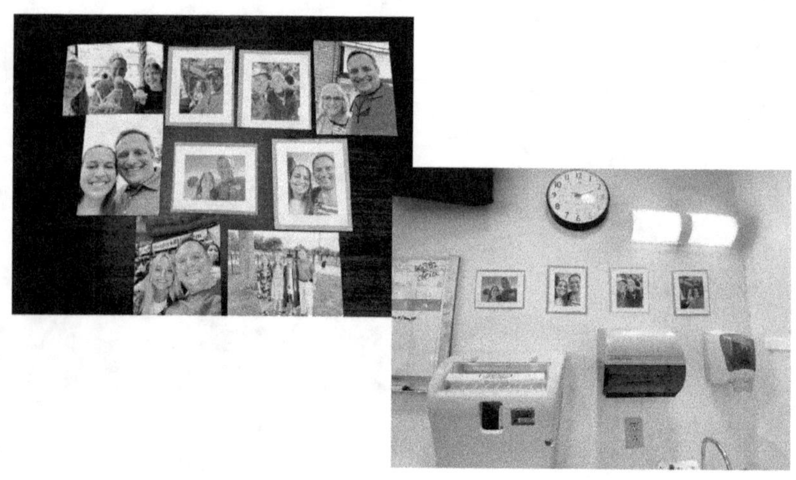

Call to Arms: Prayer Warriors: To help people see
the man they were praying for and caring for,
an ICU nurse helped Amy print and frame family
photos to hang on my hospital room wall.

Call to Arms: Prayer Warriors: Our neighbor, Joye, had a photo blanket made to hang on my hospital room wall.

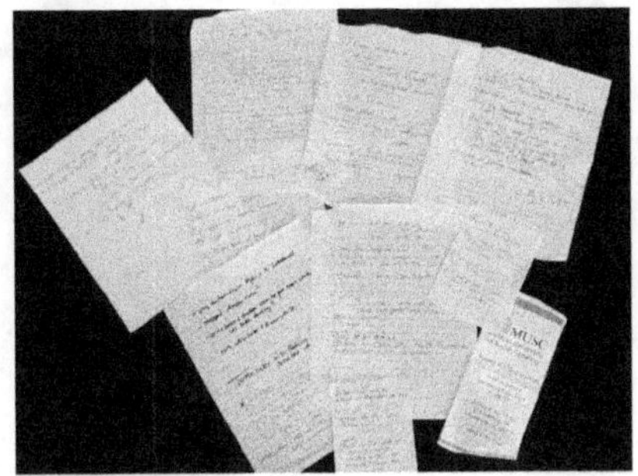

Muddy Waters: Amy kept notes of my care plan and wrote down questions for the doctor every morning.

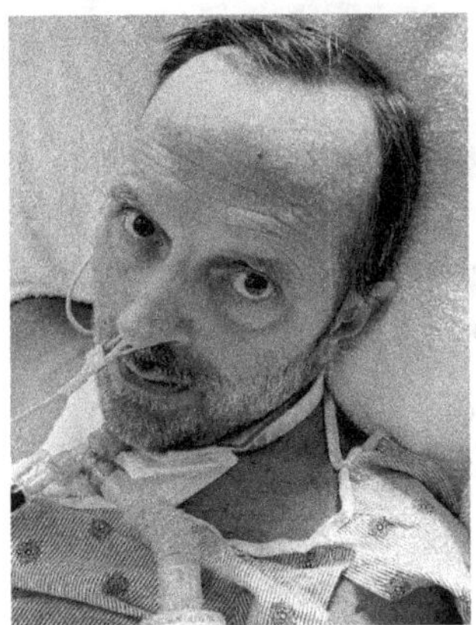

Awakening: On December 25, the gift of hope arrived when I woke up after 18 days of being unconscious.

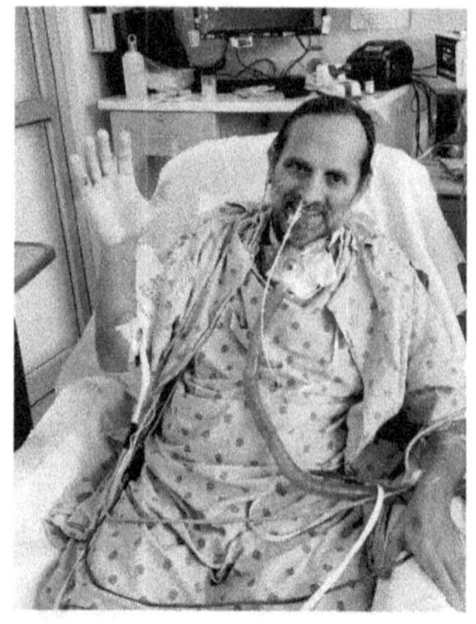

Decision: Fighting Gravity: Soon after waking up and hearing about the prayers of many, I was inspired to get out of bed and walk to the chair in my room using a cardiac walker and the support of my OT and PT team.

Decision: Fighting Gravity: Walking with a cardiac walker helped me gain confidence that I would be able to recover.

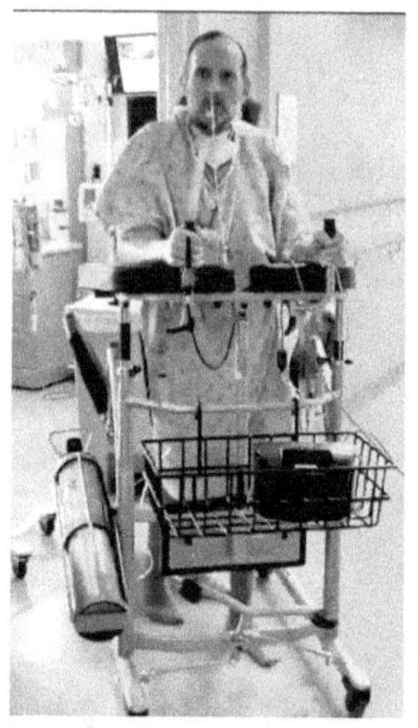

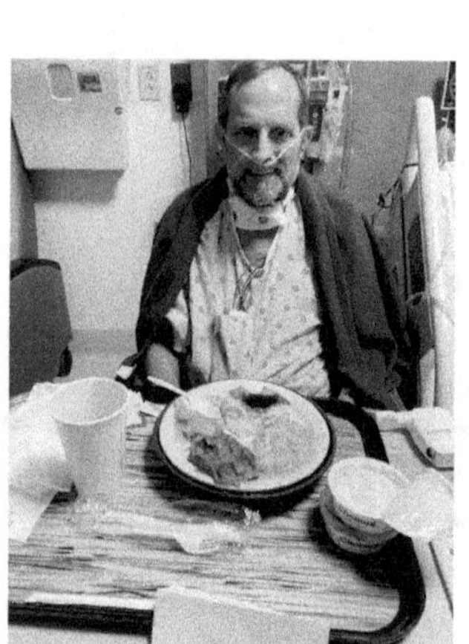

Progress and Setbacks: After relearning how to swallow and passing a swallow test, I enjoyed my first meal of pureed turkey, dressing, mashed potatoes, and green beans.

More Progress: The beard that was the subject of a vote. My wife won and I shaved it off.

Accomplishing the Goals: Amy brought me a bottle of ginger ale to celebrate passing the swallow test.

Coming Home

Coming Home: Friends stopped by when I returned home to share a meal and celebrate.

Coming Home: First Sunday back at church.

Gratitude: Amy and I standing outside my ICU room.

Amy started a daily group text with health updates and prayer reminders and included pre-cardiac arrest photos to remind everyone how full of life I was.

Kevin has been successfully converted to the lung only machine. His heart is doing OK without any heart medicine at this time which is a huge victory. Keep praying! Believing in a miracle!

So today has been a rough day. They turned off the sedation to try to wake him up. In the process he started throwing up.

They tried to give him a new pain medicine which tanked his blood pressure which led to him being put back on a heart medicine.

Now his temperature is rising so they took blood cultures to see if he has an infection in the ECMO lines or his bloodstream.

The two sites where the ECMO machine cannulas are have been oozing all day and now are bleeding.

Pray that God heals him!

Kevin is still fighting! He had a MRI yesterday that showed some findings that initially appear to be inconsequential. He is still unconscious for the most part. We are praying that God heals and protects his brain.

He had a fever during the night but they are giving him antibiotics and watching it.

His heart is doing good. They are going to keep his blood pressure lower today.

They have been able to decrease the support he needs from the ventilator.

There are no plans for additional tests or procedures for today. Hopefully today will be a day that he can rest and get better.

Please continue to pray for complete healing. Today on the way to the hospital I saw a rainbow. I saw it as a sign of hope and encouragement.

Today is day 14. They are concerned about his neurological status. He is still on a couple medicines that could affect his brain but not to the point where they can take him off those meds to get a good check. He has started moving his head today and opening his eyes more often. Pray that God protects and heals his brain.

His lungs will still take a while to heal. They are changing some things with the ventilator settings to see how much he can do on his own. There is talk of doing a tracheotomy to place a trach tube for his ventilator. That may happen in the next day or two. Pray for complete healing of his lungs

The GI bleed seems to be better.

They are still talking about days to more than a week in ICU.

Day 19:   Christmas in ICU.

Kevin had a good night. He's awake and alert this morning. They continue to make changes in his ventilator support as he is able to breathe a little better. Pray that the antibiotics take care of the bad lung infection and that God protects his lungs from any permanent damage.

Pray his heart stays strong.

Pray that God heals his whole body. Pray for miraculous healing.

Day 16:

Kevin has done well with the transition to the trach tube. They are still having to give him support with the ventilator. His lung X-ray looked better today which is a huge praise. They did a bronchoscopy and cleaned out his lungs while putting the trach in. They are also giving him Lasix to get the fluid out of his body. Pray for continued healing of his lungs.

His heart is doing well. He is having some problems with blood pressure swinging from high to low. He also has a super high ejection fraction due to the infection. Pray that his heart continues to heal and stays strong.

All sedation is off, but they are giving him pain medicine. He is alert more and can move more. He is very weak from being immobile for so long.

The last 16 days have taught me how delicate life is in the ICU. Sometimes you can recover from the heart attack but the care can cause complications too. Pray that his body stays strong to fight this infection. He has been through so much and I'm praying that this infection heals quickly and no harm comes to him because of it.

I cannot thank everyone enough for all the prayers that you have prayed for Kevin and our family. Thank you also for all the lunches and dinners you have brought me to the hospital and for all the visits. God has used you each to provide me encouragement through all this. Thank you for helping me stand in the gap for Kevin. He is worth fighting for. He is an incredible man!

Day 20:

We just saw the doctors. Kevin has had 2 runs of really fast heart beats. They are going to add a heart medicine to help control the irregular heartbeats. Pray for God to protect and heal his heart.

His lungs are about the same on X-ray. He is on a super strong antibiotic now. Pray that the lungs heal completely.

He is more alert today and able to communicate with head movements.

Pray that God heals his body completely. With each new day comes some progress, but also concerns in new areas. We still need miraculous healing!

Day 25:

Today has already been a great day. He has been on the trach collar successfully for a couple of hours. They will try a couple hours twice a day. They will increase the time on the trach collar until he no longer needs the ventilator. Once he is off of the ventilator, he can leave the ICU. It will take a while for his lungs to recover.

His heart is doing well. The cardiologist was very pleased with how well he has done this last week.

PT came today. He is very weak from being in the bed so long.

Continue to pray for complete healing and wisdom for the doctors.

There have been numerous staff that have come to visit him. One respiratory therapist told me yesterday with tears in her eyes that she was here the day they brought him in to ICU. They fought hard to save him, but were not hopeful he would make it. He is my Christmas miracle! Keep praying!!!

Day 26:

Kevin continues to improve.

The doctor told us this morning that Kevin's recovery has been amazing because at one time he was the sickest person in SC. He also told us we have a long road of recovery in front of us that could come with some bumps. He expects Kevin to be in the ICU for a bit longer and then will go to the hospital floor for a while. He also expects Kevin to have to go to a rehab facility before he can go home.

I am very tired, but so glad he continues to improve.

Please continue to pray for him and healing of his body. Pray for strength for us all.

Thanks to everyone that has rallied around our family. Thank you for all the meals you have brought to the hospital and all the support you have provided. It has been such a blessing.

MUSC has changed their visitation policy because of the increasing numbers of Covid. You cannot visit us in the hospital any longer. If anyone brings a meal, it will have to be a drop off meal.

I cannot thank everyone enough for the support!

Day 32:

As I sit and talk with my husband today, I am amazed and thankful that God performed a miracle to save him. December 7th is a day that will always be etched in my memory, but so incredibly blessed that there will be more memories with Kevin. He is an incredible man who completes me and makes me a better person.

He continues to improve. The lung CT shows improvement in his lungs. The new cardiologist is phenomenal and is really trying to get Kevin on the right medicine and make sure that everything possible is done to prevent another heart attack.

Kevin was able to walk down the hall with a stand-up walker today. He is so motivated to get stronger quickly. He is a fighter!

I cannot thank everyone enough for all the help during this difficult time. You guys have literally been the hands and feet of Jesus for our family! Keep praying for healing and endurance!

Day 37:

37 days ago we started praying for a miracle. We hoped and prayed to get to a recovery phase and here we are.

Kevin's trach tube was exchanged for a cuffless tube today. The procedure was very quick and almost painless. They will start capping trials next. Once he can go for 48 hours without needing the trach tube they can remove it.

He continues to practice his swallowing and we hope soon he will pass that test so the feeding tube can be removed.

He is getting stronger every day and can walk longer each day.

Kevin is currently getting a MRI of his heart. The cardiologist is being thorough. He wants to make sure there is not something else that caused this event.

Continue to pray for his healing and our stamina! This has been an exhausting journey, but we are both very thankful that God performed a miracle and saved Kevin's life.

Day 43:

Kevin passed the swallow test. He has no limitations on food or drinks.

He was able to walk without the walker during PT today. It is physically taxing but he did it.

The plan is still for him to be discharged on Thursday.

Continue to pray for complete healing of his body.

Day 45:

Kevin is home.

We have prayed and dreamed for this day. We are all so thankful that he is safely home!

Thank you for all the support you gave us during this difficult time. We are thankful for you all!

15

PROGRESS AND SETBACKS

Mornings were calm and quiet. I woke up to the hum of machines behind me and started to think about the day ahead.

As I gained strength, I could do a few things on my own before Amy arrived. Mainly use the bathroom, or I should say, the bedside facilities. I know it sounds gross, but it was a big deal. Although I was hooked up to everything under the sun, the fact that I could get out of bed and move to a bedside toilet was real progress.

Amy was vital to my recovery. She showed up every day. I would like to think that every spouse would do this, but I think my wife is special and heads above the rest. Even on the days she wasn't feeling well, she was not about to miss a day at the hospital, even to her own detriment. I would never have told her at the time, but I could not afford to have her miss a day with me. On one particular day, she lay on the couch in my room and took a nap for several hours. Amy was so courageous.

Others noticed her as well. One text to Amy read: "I can only imagine how depleted you must be. When I read Day 36, it struck me how long you've been maneuvering through this. You are on my mind so much throughout each day. I appreciate knowing the update each day and how to pray."

My other regular visitor, Kara, wanted me to walk twice every day. After a few days with the cardiac walker, I graduated to a standard walker. Again, progress. It really helped my soul to see myself improve. I continued to get stronger and started to walk longer distances. In the afternoons, Kara couldn't visit, so the nursing staff assisted me on these walks. It was one more item on our daily agenda, and I was all for it. Anytime I could get out of that room, walk, and see people, was fantastic.

In addition, I could sit in my chair more and Kara started me on leg exercises—standing and sitting in the chair and leg extensions, anything to regain leg strength. Eventually, Kara had me climb a couple of stairs. I cannot tell you how much I enjoyed our PT sessions every day. I could tell that Kara and Josie really wanted me to get better. Not only were they both energetic, friendly, and knowledgeable, but they really cared. It did a ton for my mental health and confidence to see and feel my progress in this area.

Not only did my legs get stronger, but my hands could now hold a phone without shaking. After a few days in step down, I was finally able to contact the outside world. Many people were praying and had sent me texts while I was unconscious in the ICU.

One series of texts came from my softball team. I was amazed at the number of texts and prayers that came from this one group. It was like having my own cheering section of fans. I was emotional reading their texts, and others from people who had reached out while I was unconscious. One text read, "I was bragging at church today about Kevin's progress and how our team rallied around him in prayer—all possible by God healing and granting our prayers. We also learned Kevin has a Rockstar Wife who has tirelessly been by his side through this entire ordeal. Character is revealed by the fire!"

To respond, I started with just a simple "Hello all," and that started a firestorm of responses. I also texted my sister-in-law on her birthday, January 9. I texted my neighbors, Joye and Jack. The responses from all of these individuals were priceless. Responses like, "This goes down as the best text ever" and "Your recovery has been an answer to so so many prayers. I don't think I've ever prayed so hard for something before."

Then came my first phone calls—my dad and my brother. All of this communication was really really special and encouraging, not only for me, but for everyone who supported me and Amy during this ordeal.

However, not everything was rosy. The time in the step-down unit also included setbacks. Each week, a "changing of the guards" meant a new group of doctors and resident physicians met in the hallway to discuss my case. On one morning, after I completed PT, doctors entered my room as normal to deliver the plan for the day. Out of the blue, as I sat in the chair and listened, I felt like I was about to pass out. I had not experienced that, besides the obvious, December 7, 2021. If you've never had this happen, imagine your field of vision becoming narrower and closing in toward the center. Then imagine losing control of your body as it starts to become limp. Fortunately, I regained control and didn't pass out. However, it was strange, especially to occur while simply sitting in a chair.

Everyone in the room noticed and I immediately let them know what had just transpired. The doctors briefly left the room to check the heart monitor's recording from the last few minutes. My heart had raced to nearly 180 bpm while at rest. That's exactly what happened when I went into cardiac arrest. It was a nervous time for me, my wife, and the staff. With no known reason for this occurrence, several things were put into place to mitigate the issue. Blood tests were done to check electrolyte levels and make adjustments, as levels were not in the normal range.

I have never wanted to be on prescription drugs long term. As my parents got older, I saw their increasing dependency on them. Every time I visited my parents' and my in-laws' homes, bottles upon bottles of prescriptions lined the counter, and I wanted no part of it. I have often said that if I were ever threatened with being on any type of blood pressure or cholesterol medicine, I would become a vegan and give up sugar. I hate the thought of being tied to prescriptions for the rest of my life. Though it is all well intended, my opinion is that once you get on one prescription, you will eventually get on many. As one drug fixes one issue, it oftentimes creates another. There are side effects and downsides, and in some cases, it can cause a spiral.

Since I was in the hospital for a cardiac arrest without a clear reason, doctors were rightfully cautious. They started me on aspirin and a statin to mitigate potential issues. I wasn't happy about it for the reasons mentioned above, but I conceded because, like the doctors, I really didn't know why my heart raced and went into cardiac arrest. After the most recent episode of my heart racing for no known reason, I started another drug, a beta-blocker. Now I was on three prescriptions, two of which I continued after I left the hospital. To me, this was a setback, but I also understand the rationale, especially for the beta-blocker. I knew I needed to take it, but I was motivated to find a way to get off of these dependencies once I left the hospital.

I wanted to go home. I was determined to accomplish a few milestones before I left the hospital that would keep me out of a rehab facility. I had to be able to walk and be strong enough to be in my own home. Amy, Kara, and I set a rigorous daily schedule to make that happen. I set a goal of walking unassisted down the ICU hallway. I wanted all the nurses and staff to see what they had accomplished. Many of them had seen me on death's door and had worked hard to save my life. It was vitally important to me that they know that their work matters. I was determined to show that to them by walking down that hallway. I wanted to give something back—encouragement and hope.

I also couldn't leave the hospital until I swallowed properly. I had failed miserably at my first swallow test in ICU. Nothing would go down the right pipe in the correct fashion. This step was important not only for my own independence, but I had first-hand experience with feeding tubes and mentally, I was not interested in living that way.

Years prior, unfortunately my mother's brain hemorrhage paralyzed her left side for the remainder of her life. She spent the first four months in a hospital and rehab facility before my father brought her home to care for her. Prior to going home, she could not swallow correctly, so she had to have a percutaneous endoscopic gastrostomy (PEG) tube surgically placed into her stomach. To feed her, we had to pour a liquid diet into the tube each day.

I was fearful that I may never regain my ability to swallow and enjoy eating like most people do. To me, a PEG tube and having my family feed me a liquid diet, just feels like the end—that I would never get better and might as well give up. I didn't want this to happen to me. I wanted to get better and restore my life.

To help with this, a speech therapist worked with me to improve my ability to swallow. The therapist gave me tips and exercises, primarily using ice chips. After a few days, the therapist decided to give me another shot at the swallow test. I was wheeled to the testing area and moved to a chair adjacent to the X-ray machine. Just like the first test, I was asked to swallow a liquid. Once again, I failed.

I was frustrated. I needed to pass this test. I met with the speech therapist again, along with a few doctors. The possibility of esophageal damage was presented, as it could have narrowed during my hospital stay and might be contributing to food being diverted into my lungs. This could have happened from the insertion of the trach and the trauma of my cardiac arrest. Having my esophagus expanded might be of benefit to regain swallow function, so I agreed to this surgery. Once again, I was wheeled to an operating room, placed under anesthesia, and the doctors expanded my throat. It was a quick procedure, lasting less than 15 minutes and I was awake again in no time. Within a day of the procedure, I could tell it helped, but I didn't think it would be the total answer. I was relegated to chewing and swallowing ice chips. My swallowing was definitely not normal yet.

One morning, I woke up early with one thing on my mind—learn to swallow. As an engineer by trade, I thought about the mechanics of swallowing. I don't consider myself a really good analytical engineer, but at times, I can dive into the analytical world. For my entire life, I had never given a thought to how to swallow, it just came naturally. But that day, I thought about how the throat and tongue have to operate for a person to swallow. When you swallow, your tongue pushes the food or drink to the back of your mouth, triggering a reflex that closes off the airway while the throat muscles contract to move the food down the esophagus.

So, utilizing my own saliva, I sat in bed and practiced this sequence of events. I started to get the feel of forcing my tongue to the back of my throat. It was not natural. Then, I concentrated on squeezing the top part of my throat, followed by squeezing the bottom part of my throat. Again, not natural. In the dark hours of the morning, again and again, I repeated the whole sequence. First the tongue, then the esophagus. It was as if God woke me up and said, "Kevin, today you are going to learn how to swallow again." As I sat there that morning and put it all together, I began to think I had a breakthrough.

On Friday, January 14, the speech therapist visited again. I had been cleared to leave the hospital the following Thursday, if I passed another swallow test on Tuesday, January 18. If I didn't pass, I would leave with a PEG tube. I was determined. For the next few days, I practiced and practiced the mechanics of swallowing. I told the therapist about my practice sessions. She felt my throat and observed me while I demonstrated the exercises. After a quick session, she looked at me and said, "How do you feel about doing another swallow test just to see how you are doing in preparation for the one coming up on Tuesday?" Even though I felt like I would fail, I was up for it. I, too, wanted to see if I had made any progress.

As before, the test began with a liquid. I took the cup, thought through the mechanics of swallowing, and attempted to swallow. As I did, I tried to catch a peek at the monitor and see the staff's faces. I heard some discussion but couldn't make out what was said. Then, the speech therapist gave me another cup with a different liquid. Once again, I thought through the mechanics of swallowing and proceeded to swallow. I didn't know how I was doing, but I stayed focused on the mechanics. She then gave me another type of liquid.

My expectation for this practice test before the real test on Tuesday was to just get a progress update. To say I was surprised by the results would be an understatement. I had partially passed the swallow test and could have my feeding tube removed. I had improved enough to go on a soft food diet. To have my feeding tube removed was a huge moment. It gave me hope that maybe I could get my life back.

I was wheeled back to my room. Once there, I sat on the donut pillow in the chair and shared the good news with Amy. It was a big victory, but I had to improve before the real test on Tuesday. The speech therapist returned to discuss the details of the next few days. We reviewed my new 100 percent pureed food diet and I was instructed to be very careful when eating. Everything would be blended to a consistency similar to the swallow test. All of my practice to relearn how to swallow would be needed to ensure I did not aspirate the food.

I took a deep breath and the long feeding tube was pulled out through my nose. The technician removed the sutures that held it in place. The last time it was removed was to confirm that the tube was free of metal in preparation for an MRI, but this time, it stayed out. Not a great experience, but it was the last time I had to deal with that.

The next order of business was to choose my dinner from a menu! I was like a kid in a candy store. It was like reading a menu for the very first time. You may be reading my story and think nothing of it, you've probably selected from a menu a thousand times. But for me, every event like this one was a huge event. I looked over the pureed section and made a decision: pureed turkey, dressing, mashed potatoes, and green beans. I guess since I had missed Christmas dinner and did not remember Thanksgiving, I was making up for lost time.

When the food arrived, they set my first "meal" on the mobile table in front of my chair. I sat up and opened the tray. There it was—100 percent pureed food. I could identify each food only by its color. The stuffing and mashed potatoes had gravy on top. The green beans were...well green, and then, there was the beige turkey.

The moment of truth—the first bite. I placed a small portion in my mouth and swallowed as I had practiced. Most of you have no idea what this moment was like. All I can say is that it had to be the best food I had ever tasted in my life! Even though I had a ways to go, it was a huge victory. An unexpected victory at that. Tasting food, pureed and all, was one of the better moments of my life. Certainly not the best, but it was high on the list. It was as if I knew in that moment that I had experienced a breakthrough and I was going to be okay.

The first time I ate, the speech therapist stayed with me to ensure I had no issues. Before each bite I thought through the mechanics of swallowing. I took each bite very slowly to ensure I swallowed properly. To help wash it all down, I was given water with a thickener added to it, but I was only allowed small sips.

I've reflected on this moment, and a couple things come to mind to ponder. First, oftentimes it is hard to relate to someone who is going through an illness that lands them in the hospital. I hope though, that the details of my story give you a sense of what it is like to be a patient, and that you gain more empathy for those in a similar situation.

While it's tough on family and caregivers, it's also tough for the patient—tough physically, but really tough mentally. Immobile most of the time, the patient is captured by their thoughts. Our thoughts can be good, and they can be bad. And when they are bad, they are bad.

Second, I think at times, it is really important to get quiet and listen for guidance that only comes when we block out the noise of our world. In this case, listen for the voice of God. The world is chaotic and wants nothing more than to distract you. That is why you have to be intentional about getting quiet, disconnecting from what the world offers, and listen for His voice. That is when breakthroughs can really happen.

16

MORE PROGRESS

The day I would get to go home was near. But I still had a trach inserted into my neck. The trach collar was helpful for my speech, but to be fully removed was a complicated process.

Every few days, an X-ray tech came to my room, placed a hard board behind my back and took a picture of my lungs to help doctors monitor my severe lung infection and determine if I was ready for a trach reduction. The heavy dose of antibiotics improved the infection, but it took four months to completely heal.

As mentioned, my first trach reduction test in the ICU was so painful, and was one of the few unpleasant experiences while in the hospital. However, in the step-down unit, two additional reduction tests were executed with no issues. Each time after, my oxygen levels were constantly monitored to ensure I was breathing on my own.

Along with the trach reductions, I was introduced to a neat tool called a speaking valve, another step to ween me off the trach and supplemental oxygen. The external trach cannulas were removed and the valve was placed onto the trach itself. This accomplished two things: It took me fully off of trach support and supplemental oxygen and it allowed me to speak more normally.

The first time the valve was placed was a wild experience. I could talk more normally; however, I felt like I was suffocating. I wasn't, but it felt like it. I hung in there for a while, but eventually I asked for the valve to be removed. It was a good first step, but maybe too large of a step.

I used the speaking valve on a periodic basis to talk to someone, but I could remove it when I was alone or needed to rest. It was one step closer to having the trach capped and then removed. Just like practicing swallowing ice chips and exercising my legs throughout the day, the speaking valve was another process to restore my life.

After one more trach reduction while using the speaking valve, the staff was comfortable with capping the trach. I was then monitored for a couple of days. I did fantastic. My lungs had improved enough to breathe without the trach support, but with the occasional use of supplemental oxygen through my nose. My lungs were now in good enough shape to have the trach removed.

On January 15, just one day after partially passing the swallow test, the trach was removed. A visible hole in my throat required a lot of attention for it to close and heal. It was cleaned and bandaged, but over the next few days the bandage became soiled regularly and had to be changed. If I coughed or spoke with any force, the bandage became dislodged. So, I got in the habit of holding onto it anytime I spoke—a minor inconvenience. It took a couple of weeks for the hole to close entirely, so it required constant monitoring even after I returned home.

I was now free to move around my room. The trach and the feeding tube were removed, as if the "seat belt signs were turned off." Only a heart monitor connected me to the bed now, and it could easily be disconnected. This meant I was finally able to accomplish the task that I was so focused on when I first woke up in ICU—use a regular toilet. After five weeks, I could now do something that most folks normally do without a thought. However, for me, it was another big deal. No longer would anyone have to clean up after me. Progress!

Being able to move to the bathroom also meant I had access to the bathroom mirror. I took a good look at myself. I knew I had grown a pretty good beard, but I was not prepared to see the person staring back at me.

I could not believe what I looked like. I was skin and bones. It was crazy how much muscle mass I had lost. I wasn't a body builder to begin with, but most of the muscle I did have was pretty much gone. Even though I had lost a lot of weight in muscle mass and "padding" on my tail, I had a small belly. Can you believe that? I lost muscle, but I had fat around my stomach! Couldn't my body have just left my muscle alone and used up the fat around my stomach?

Every night in step down, the staff woke me up every four hours to check my blood pressure and heart rate. Even at 4:00 a.m. every morning, they woke me up for one task—get out of bed and stand on a scale. Nothing like getting a full uninterrupted night's sleep! It was 4:00 a.m., not 7:00 a.m., not 8:00 a.m., but 4:00 a.m. I understand it was necessary to ensure I was getting enough nutrition through the feeding tube, but the hour never made sense to me. It was explained to me that a person is at their lowest weight at 4:00 a.m. I can't imagine I gained a tremendous amount of weight between 4:00 a.m. and 7:00 a.m., but whatever.

Regardless, through this exercise, I was surprised by how much weight I lost—34 pounds!

Now that I could walk to the bathroom, gone were the days of washcloth baths and dry shampoo while lying in the bed. The flexibility afforded me a nice option—a sink bath. The soap suds on my hair and body made me start to feel like a human being again. But another thing needed to happen before I looked like myself again.

I don't have facial hair on a regular basis, I've been clean shaven for over 35 years. However, after being unconscious with limited mobility for six weeks, I looked like Rip Van Winkle. I had woken up with a fully-grown beard.

So, like any normal guy, I polled the female nurses on if they liked the beard. For comparison, I showed them pictures on my walls of me without a beard. Without any doubt or dissension, even with some gray hair mixed in, all of the nurses liked the beard. Except...my wife did not. She claimed that it made me look old. Whatever. In the end, I shaved it off. Another benefit of being free to move around the room and utilize the bathroom sink and mirror.

17

ACCOMPLISHING THE GOALS

The TV was off. It would not help me with my goals. In the final week at the hospital, I was focused on two key items—swallow completely and walk unassisted. These two accomplishments would allow me to return home and avoid a rehab facility.

Amy and I committed to the daily plan. Every day was focused and busy. We made our list of questions to ask, I strengthened my legs with daily PT sessions, and I continued my daily regimen of swallowing exercises. In addition, I had extra visits from doctors and additional tests and X-rays.

To strengthen my legs, Kara always left me exercises to complete: stand up and sit down in the chair, do leg extensions and slight squats, and climb a couple of stairs. Eventually, I became strong enough that the nurses were comfortable with Amy assisting me on walks. I could now use a regular walker, but was starting to ween myself. To do that, Amy pushed the walker while I held on to it next to her with one hand. After a few days, I could walk the unit a couple of times without the walker. It was quite comical, but also encouraging to see Amy push the walker next to me as if she was the one who needed it. I knew I was getting better.

In my last weekend at the hospital, I focused on my fourth swallow test that would be conducted that Tuesday. For extra practice, it helped that I could eat pureed food now. With each bite, I thought about the parts of my mouth and throat and how their functions send food in the right direction. I took my time to ensure I didn't aspirate. It was an arduous process, but I had to build this muscle. I wanted to go home.

When the day and time finally arrived for my fourth test, I was anxious. It was like taking a final college exam. The results would determine if I went home. I have never wanted to pass a test so badly in my life. I was wheeled to the testing area. My mind was locked in, I was in the zone. I visualized the correct way to swallow and told myself that I would pass this test 100 percent. Over and over, I went through the sequence.

When it was time for the test, I sat in front of an X-ray machine and they gave me a progression of items to swallow—thick liquids, followed by thin liquids, then cookies, etc. With each bite I stayed focused and executed my practice. I couldn't think about anything else. I would carry this sequence along until they told me to stop. As we proceeded further into the test than I ever had, I kept my emotions in check. I didn't let the progression distract me.

Then it stopped. No additional items were given. I sat there in anticipation of the results, and then, the moment came. The speech therapist looked at me and said what I had wanted to hear for a couple of weeks...I passed! No more restrictions on what I ate, no PEG tube, but most importantly, no barrier in this area stood in the way of me going home. It was as if I had just won an Olympic gold medal.

I returned to my room and told Amy the good news. After

that, there was only one thing I wanted to do—drink ginger ale, something I craved since being in the ICU. Since those days, I knew that once I could swallow fully, the first thing I wanted to do was drink ginger ale. But this time it wouldn't be swabbed in my mouth or eaten as ice chips. On the day of my swallow test, Amy brought me my very own bottle of ginger ale in anticipation of me passing. So, just like many people celebrate with a bottle of champagne, I broke open that bottle of ginger ale and drank it. That was a celebration!

Texts of encouragement continued, "Kevin you have been doing so awesome. Keep moving toward the end goal. God has answered numerous prayers for you and Amy. Praise God and can't wait to see you again."

After the celebration, I ordered my first regular meal. Although I had really enjoyed the pureed food, it was time to graduate to solid foods. My first meal was a stir fry bowl with brown rice. It was fantastic. I had finally accomplished the swallowing goal, but one goal remained.

It had been two weeks since I stood for the first time. Now, I could walk around the step-down unit without the walker, but I utilized it at times for balance. I was pretty weak, but for the most part, my ability to walk on my own was going well. A big hurdle was to climb stairs, but soon, I climbed the practice set of stairs with no issues. My confidence grew and so did my outlook on being able to have a life outside of the hospital. Thankfully, Kara became comfortable with my progress. This was important since she would need to agree to let me go home. Since she was monitoring me on a regular basis, her agreement came without any issues.

But I had a personal goal in mind before I left the hospital—walk unassisted down the ICU hallway. It was important to me that the ICU staff see the results of their hard work.

They have a tough job, one that doesn't always end well. I knew that seeing a patient recover after 30 days in the ICU would be an encouragement and I wanted to give it to them.

Kara was on board with the plan and we agreed to accomplish it the day before I left the hospital. To celebrate, Amy brought in four dozen single bundtlets from Nothing Bundt Cakes to give to the staff. Ironic that a heart patient would hand out dessert, but I knew they would appreciate it.

On Wednesday morning, the day we would surprise the ICU staff, Kara arrived to my room with a wheelchair and a walker. To save my energy, I rode in the wheelchair to the elevator and went down to the ICU floor. Once I got to the ICU department doors, I would walk and only use the walker if needed.

The double doors to the ICU opened. I stood from the wheelchair and began to walk down the hallway. I recognized some people, but some were new to me. I walked slowly. At first, it was business as usual, but then someone noticed me, and then another. Word spread and by the time I got to the nurse's station, a crowd had formed. Although the staff recognized me, they really knew Amy. They hugged us both. A number of them choked up and cried when they saw me. They were elated to see me in this condition. It was just as I had hoped.

A few of the nurses introduced themselves. Two in particular were there on December 7 when I arrived. They explained how severe my situation was and that they were amazed to see me now. Not only had I survived, but I was walking and in pretty good shape. They also spoke of Amy's courage during that time.

I stayed as long as I could, hugging and chatting with the staff. I took my time to encourage them and tell them that their work really does matter. They need this. When a family member goes into the hospital, particularly the ICU, it is hard on the family. But it is also hard on the staff. Yes, it is their job, and they are trained to handle this type of situation, but they are also humans. They have feelings and emotions—they truly care. It can take a toll. I'm glad I was able to give something back to them—encouragement, hope, and friendship. I will always be grateful for their part in saving my life.

18

COMING HOME

On Thursday, January 20, after 45 days in the hospital, I could go home. It was a big day. For over a week, I had been told this would be the day, and I had worked through hurdles to make it happen. With the help of many people in and out of the hospital, I accomplished all of the necessary goals. I could walk and eat, and I was fitted with an external defibrillator. I had all of my prescriptions and instructions. I just needed my discharge paperwork and a wheelchair ride out of the hospital.

I cleaned myself up, strapped the defibrillator to my chest, and got dressed. I also visited the first floor of the hospital to be fitted with a heart monitor, which I had to wear for another month. My bags were packed and I was ready to go.

After lunch, hospital transportation arrived to my room with a wheelchair for a ride down the elevator. The trip through the hospital and outside its doors was surreal. I had been in a hospital room for so long that outside felt new and differ-ent—a weird feeling.

It wasn't long before Amy pulled the car up and I was helped into the passenger seat. We were on our way. Just like the departure trip through the hospital, the drive home felt weird.

The car ride, traffic, signs, buildings, bridges—it was almost new again. It was a beautiful day, the bright sky was striking.

I looked forward to being home. Around 3:00 p.m., we pulled into our neighborhood and drove down the main road. Amy made the right-hand turn onto our street, Rees Row, and I immediately noticed a few things. The school bus was there and our niece, Sarah, would be stepping off of it. In addition, to celebrate my return, red balloons were on every mailbox and many of our neighbors were on the street to welcome me home.

That's when I spotted Joye. I asked Amy to stop the car so I could get out. I had waited for this moment. I was going to do it right then and there—my first hug was for Joye. I walked to her and gave her the best hug that I possibly could. That was a special moment.

Joye and I will be forever connected. She is my lifesaver and words cannot describe how grateful I am. I have been able to continue my life on earth because of her. Had she not responded that day, I would not have been able to make incredible memories. I am a husband, a father, a brother, a son, an uncle, and a friend. One day, I may even be a grandparent. Joye is a big reason for that.

After I hugged and thanked Joye, I made my way to other neighbors for more hugs. Even the kids on our street were there to welcome me home. We stood at the end of our street for a few more minutes until I started to get tired. I walked back to the car, it was time to go home. As we approached our driveway, I noticed two things. Written at the end of our driveway in chalk, were the words "Rees Row Miracle." And, a banner hung from our porch, "Welcome home Kevin, We missed you." All of our neighbor's names were on it. As I made my way to the front steps of our home, more neighbors met me there. We chatted for a few moments before my legs began to shake. I only had a few more minutes before I would be too tired to climb the 15 stairs to the front door.

Amy and I slowly made our way up to the porch. This was a significant moment, and our neighbors captured it by taking pictures of me and Amy standing on the stair landing. I look back at those pictures today with joy. What an incredible moment that was.

As I entered our home, it was quiet. I slowly took in the surroundings—it was surreal and strange to be back in my own home. I recognized everything, but it was as if I had never lived there. In some ways, it was new. I made my way onto the back porch and sat down. It was a gorgeous January day—sunny and warm. I sat and listened to the birds and gazed out into nature. I sat there for an hour to process all that I had just gone through.

Later that evening, friends, Liz and Brown brought us dinner. Liz had been one of the many sources of encouragement for Amy. She prayed some of the most beautiful prayers on my behalf. That night, we ate dinner together, just as we had on December 4. We had spent a couple hours together just days before my cardiac arrest, but all I could remember of that night was that they left in a Jeep. As we talked over dinner on my first night home, bits and pieces returned to my memory.

A number of events prior to December 7 had left my memory. Even today, memories from the days leading up to my cardiac arrest have not returned. However, as time has passed and as people have spoken about these events, my memory has somewhat returned. Over the next few days following my return home, we had a number of visitors. Although I was weak, I always welcomed our friends at the front door. One day, I shocked Sam and Joan when I opened the front door to greet them. Seeing me standing in front of them at the entrance to our home brought them joy and amazement. Jim and Janet came over to watch an NFL playoff game and we enjoyed an evening with Dan and Patty.

A number of neighbors and friends brought us food. I always asked each of them to stay and eat with us, but not all did, so we ended up with a freezer full of food. This was fantastic as I was definitely underweight at the time. I soon learned that the gift of food was nothing new to our family. While I was in the hospital, many friends, church members, and neighbors brought meals to Amy in the hospital, GrubHub, gift cards to feed my girls, or blessed them with cash for necessities. The list is long. I may leave someone out if I try to name everyone.

A number of items needed to be fixed in our home. Steve and Janet came over with food and stayed to work on my garage door and fill up the bird feeder. Kevin and Scott from my men's Bible study small group came over with pizza and replaced my closet light. They also had Chick-Fil-A delivered a couple of times to Amy while I was in the hospital. My neighbor Jack kept our yard clean.

Other friends came to sit with me. Hal, Brett, Mark, Mike, Eisaku, Brian, Dustin and Annissa...the list goes on and on. I was overwhelmed with how many visitors came to see me. I often just sat in a chair with a blanket over me and chatted with them. At one point, I told my dad about how grateful I was that so many people came to see me. I have never forgotten his response, "Kevin, always remember, you have to be a friend to have a friend." I had never thought about that fact. I had sowed into these relationships and I was now reaping the benefits. It reminds me of how important it is to pour into people's lives and to be a part of a community, whether it is a church, Bible study small group, or other close-knit groups. You never know when you might need them.

Another important thing to me after I arrived home on a

Thursday was to attend church that Sunday. Just like my intent to walk down the ICU hallway before I left the hospital, I wanted to walk into church the Sunday after I arrived home. A lot of people had prayed for me and a lot of them would be at church. I wanted to see them, but I also wanted them to see me. I was grateful for their support and being at church would be a tremendous encouragement for me and for each of them.

So, on Sunday, I walked in with my rollator walker, sort of undercover. We sat in the lower left-hand side of the church. As soon as church let out, I began to see friends. Outside of the sanctuary, we made our way around to see many of our friends, until we met up with Pastor Michael Morris. Within minutes he whisked me and Amy to a room to see the pastoral staff. Pastor Josh Surratt had just given the message, and when I walked into that room, it lit up. Several of the staff and their families were present. It was a very special time for everyone. Before we left, we took a picture with Josh, and was led in prayer by Pastor Josh Walters, who was dripping wet from conducting a baptism.

Word spread that I had returned home and those first few days can be summed up by the responses that poured in. "I have prayed so many times that his complete recovery would baffle the medical community. Your faith, Amy...it has truly inspired and changed me. Kevin was healed by faith."

Another read, "His progress so far is nothing short of a miracle! I know he has weeks of hard work to go still, but God will be there with him. This has been good for me to witness Kevin's miracle! I'm so happy for you both."

And another, "God is in control! This is a Big Amen Story! All of our Faith should have been strengthened by Kevin's journey!"

19

DRIVE TO HEALING

The excitement of being home was dying down, and it was time to get into a routine. Now that I was home, I could do a little more to regain my strength. I was weak, and there was no better indicator than my inability to do a pushup. I had regular in-home visits from occupational and physical therapy and in-home nurses came to help me continue the work that had been done in the hospital.

The PT nurse arrived, did an assessment, and gave me a list of exercises to do each day. This included body weight exercises and going from sitting to standing from a chair. In addition, I did leg lifts and squats with bands. One exercise involved climbing the 14 steps to the second level of our home. With my Fitbit on my wrist and a finger monitor to check my heart rate, I slowly climbed until I reached the top. I periodically checked my heart rate, which routinely exceeded 100bpm. Even more astounding was how out of breath I became. It was as if I had just sprinted a 40-yard dash. The depth of my breathing was pretty shallow as my lungs were recovering from trauma. Eventually, I worked my way up to a few ascensions each time.

Another way to regain my strength was to walk our street with the rollator walker. Amy carried it down the steps and into the driveway and then I walked to the end of the street and back. The great thing about the rollator is the built-in seat for when I got tired—something I had learned from watching my dad use one. I walked every day and soon found that I didn't need the rollator anymore.

It wasn't until the last set of exercises on the floor that I realized the full extent of my weakness. I rotated from my back to my belly and tried to push myself up off of the ground. But, I couldn't—not one pushup. I was amazed. To get off the ground I had to scoot myself to the couch and pull myself up. I got a sense of what elderly folks must go through if they ever find themselves in this position. It was a very humbling and insightful experience.

To strengthen my upper body, I turned to bands. It was an easy, efficient way to begin the process. Every day, I used them to do bicep curls, shoulder presses, and chest exercises. It wasn't long though before I realized that my right shoulder was still not right. Ultimately, I felt the full effects of the pain at the end of 2022 and had shoulder surgery in early 2023 to repair extensive damage.

Another thing to manage during these early days at home was my external defibrillator. After about two months, I had regained enough strength and my lungs had healed enough for surgery to place an implantable cardioverter defibrillator (ICD). In the meantime, I had to wear a defibrillator vest and lug around a battery pack, and I had to wear a heart monitor in the middle of my chest. These things, though valuable at the time, required a lot of management and maintenance. It was quite a chore to sleep.

One nuance of the defibrillator was the threat of "therapy" from a false reading. "Therapy" means that it would shock the heck out of you to restore a normal heart rhythm. The machine gives a 15 second warning and if you don't discontinue the advancement of the therapy, well... The entire time I wore the vest, I never had an actual "therapy" event; however, I had numerous false readings—a few in the middle of the night. Let me tell you, there is nothing like getting woken up from a dead sleep by an alarm that only has a matter of seconds to avert an unintended shock.

Unstable when standing for long periods of time, I used a shower chair to prevent falls. Before I could shower, I had to remove the external defibrillator and heart monitor, which made for an anxious time for Amy. Although unlikely to go into a VFib while in the shower, I would be unprotected for a short period of time. So, I would not be left unattended while cleaning myself up.

In those first few weeks at home, my legs weren't the only weak parts of my body. My swallow, though capable, was difficult. Even though I had passed the swallow test, I needed to be careful. I had to eat very slowly. I also paid attention to the consistency of the food and stuck to food that was easily digestible—nothing tough or hard to break apart. My appetite was developing as well.

Within a couple of weeks, I returned to the hospital for cardiac rehab. I was excited to start more advanced exercises and see how my heart responded to light cardio. It began with an interview process so the staff could better understand what happened and assess my current condition. From there, they designed a workout regimen to help build my strength. Visits would be three times per week for one hour at a time.

At each visit, another cardiac monitor was attached to my body to give real-time feedback to the staff while I exercised. They checked my vitals before I started. The workout usually included five or six exercises to perform over the hour. I tracked my progress on paper, including the effort needed to conduct the exercise and any issues involved with completing the exercise. Several patients worked out together, which made it feel like a family-type environment. I got to know the staff and some of my fellow patients. Over time, I progressed to more advanced exercises, including the elliptical and ultimately, running on a treadmill. All in all, I spent three months in cardiac rehab and it did a tremendous amount of good for both my physical and mental well-being. It gave me confidence that I could recover.

I wanted to get better, but I also really wanted to see my family. Both of my daughters were in college and my father still lived near Raleigh. Just like I wanted to go to church and see my friends, I couldn't wait to see my family.

The second weekend after getting home, Amy and I made a two-hour day trip to see my oldest daughter, Reagan. I sat on a donut pillow in the car to help get my thin body comfortable. We ate with her at our favorite Indian restaurant. But my favorite part of that trip was walking down the sidewalk arm in arm with my daughter to get takeout from another restaurant I liked. I was too weak to walk on my own, but she held onto me. A highlight of the trip.

In March, Amy and I traveled to Houston for her own doctor appointment. It was quite an experience to go through airport security with an external defibrillator. Nothing like security pulling you aside to check out the vest strapped to your body with a black box attached. However, it was a good trip. We saw several former coworkers, who are also friends of mine.

We also took a trip to see my father. On this particular trip though, we had to visit him in the hospital after he had fallen ill. It was good for us to be there not only to see him, but to meet with the doctors and make a plan to handle an ongoing fluid retention kidney issue. Little did I know at the time, this would be an arduous journey for him. We lost him the following year.

The trip to Raleigh took a turn for the worse at home. While we visited my father, we received a phone call from our neighbor who was watching our house and animals. Our dog, Grace, had developed a disabling condition and had to be taken to the emergency vet. We returned home to learn that she had developed an issue with her spine and she would not recover. We made the difficult decision to let her go. It is really hard to lose family members, but it is also hard to lose a family pet. My neighbors were great and helped me bury Grace.

Over the next two weeks, I mentally prepared for ICD surgery. Soon, I would be free of the external defibrillator. I was not crazy about having an implanted defibrillator, especially since there was no explanation for what caused the VFib in the first place. But it seemed prudent to have this safety device in my body in the event it happened again. I tried not to think about what they had to do to my heart while in surgery. Once the surgeon installed the defibrillator, he would need to replicate a scenario to ensure it would work. This meant that my heart would need to race to a point that required the defibrillator to administer a "therapy" and shock the heck out of me. Obviously, I would be asleep, but I really didn't want my heart to go through this again. But it had to be done to complete the objective. In the end, the surgery and recovery went well.

The last big trip was flying to Nashville to see Caroline, and my brother and sister-in-law. We hadn't visited them since my daughter transferred colleges. I had also never visited my brother since he moved to Nashville, so this was an exciting trip. We spent a few days exploring Caroline's college, eating at a number of restaurants, visiting a few coffee shops, and taking in a Predators hockey game.

Over the course of three months, I processed my physical healing. I also tried to get back to a somewhat normal life. Or at least, a new normal with daily routines. I took daily walks again on the golf course, attended church, and visited with family and friends. Questions remained as to why this all happened, but I was determined to heal—physically, mentally, and spiritually.

20

GRATITUDE

While I was in the hospital, I did my best to thank everyone—nurses, doctors, techs, pastors, friends, family. You name it. It was very important to me to show my deep gratitude for the individuals who cared for me. I know that everyone plays a part, but they don't always have someone thank them for what they do. I wanted to be different. And in a way, maybe they would see Christ through me.

That was why it was so important for me to walk down the ICU hallway. I wanted to encourage them, but I also wanted to show my gratitude. It makes a difference. Who knows how my efforts that day inspired someone to keep going in the face of adversity, suffering, or even death. God knows, but my job that day was to give something back to that staff.

At home, the same applied to Joye and Jack and everyone who responded on December 7. Within days of getting home, I began an effort to identify all of the individuals who had been in my home that day. Joye knew people who worked in the Charleston County Emergency Department, so I enlisted her help. While Joye was on the phone with the county coordinator to identify the personnel, one of the paramedics who responded to my emergency that day was in the coordinator's office. When he heard that I was the subject of the phone call, and that I was alive, he could not believe it.

We were able to identify the on-scene commander, the paramedics, and the firefighters from the two stations within a couple of miles of our home. Once I got their names, I worked with Joye and the coordinator on a plan to meet everyone. The "A" shift had been on the day I went into cardiac arrest. I learned that their next day shift would be on Valentine's Day, so Amy and I planned a surprise visit to the two stations for that day. We picked up treats for them at Nothing Bundt Cakes.

Our first stop was Station 4. Amy and I walked in and asked for the individuals who responded that day. Three of them were there, and to say they were shocked is an understatement. They remembered me and recalled specifics from that day. We chatted and took a few pictures with them.

It is hard to put into words how I felt in that moment. In front of me, were three individuals who saved my life. Since I was unconscious, I don't have a recollection of the event. As they shared details, I tried to compute them in my brain and have it make sense—it's difficult. I felt such thankfulness. I left them with the treats, but more importantly, I left them with a sense of gratitude for all they did to save my life.

Our next stop was Station 6. We met with the first responders, and just like at Station 4, we had a great visit. They recalled that day and remembered the details and sequence of events. One paramedic was not present, but we reached him by phone. Later, after a video of my healing journey was played at church during the Easter service, he walked up to me with his wife to introduce himself.

In late February, we made our last stop. Joye had contacted the county supervisor and arranged a meeting with two of the paramedics who had responded in the ambulance, the on-scene commander, and the 911 call center ladies who had answered the call. This was also a great opportunity for the county supervisor to educate people on the benefits of learning CPR, and promote the necessary classes to learn this skill. Several news agencies were invited to the meeting. We arrived at the County Emergency Medical Services building where we were escorted to a large room. Then, we had the opportunity to meet all of the folks who were instrumental in saving my life on December 7, 2021.

I met the on-scene commander, the first person to arrive after Joye and the last person to leave that day. We also met the two paramedics who transported me to the hospital, who informed me that I had breathed on my own during that drive, and had even awakened a couple of times. They kept up with my status and progress during the first few days I was in the hospital.

During that meeting, we also met the four ladies who worked in the call center. This was not only a special moment for me, but also for Amy. One of the women we met had spent a lot of time talking to Amy during my cardiac arrest, keeping her as calm as possible.

I know it sounds redundant, but it was surreal to talk to all of these individuals. They had seen me at my very worst. They had seen Amy at her very worst. For me, hearing their side of the story continued to make it more real for me. Of course I recalled everything from the hospital after I had awakened, but hearing more details about December 7 really brought it home. It was one more step in my journey to wrap my head around everything that had happened to me.

Later in 2022, I returned to the same ICU floor at MUSC. This time, I was there to support one of Amy's friends. Her husband was in a similar situation as I had been. He was on ECMO, and his room was right next to the one where I had spent 30 days. While I was there to offer encouragement, I also had the opportunity to see several of the nurses who had cared for me, including some who were there the day I arrived.

From my conversations with them, I learned more about how severe and dire my situation had been. Just like the visit with the firefighters and paramedics, it was surreal. Even though I had heard a lot by this point, details from the nurses who were in the emergency room that day made it even more real. It was as if someone opened a picture book and showed me a time in my life that I could not recall. They were all thankful and amazed at my survival and recovery. More importantly, it deepened my thankfulness for all they had done that day.

In January 2023, I once again paid a visit to the ICU staff. This time, I was invited to speak to the whole department about my survival, recovery, and experiences in the hospital. Many in attendance didn't have first-hand experience with my case. I also took this opportunity to show my gratitude and provide encouragement to the entire team.

Speaking to a group of people who often deal with tragedies, death, and discouragement gave me a deeper appreciation for their roles in saving my life. I wanted to do my best to tell them that their jobs really do matter and that sometimes there can be a happy ending. I did not expect how much I would be impacted mentally after sharing my experiences with them. Things do not always work out like they did for me, but I hope that I gave a bit of hope to each one of them.

I would be remiss if I did not mention this within the chapter titled, Gratitude:

First, I would like to thank everyone who prayed for my survival and recovery. I have already mentioned a number of folks already, but there were many others who don't even know me personally who prayed out of faith.

Second, I would like to thank everyone who supported

Amy and my family through this. You unselfishly put yourself forward to do things that were inconvenient and sometimes difficult. You made sacrifices that you had not planned for in advance.

Third, I would like to thank my family for all of your support. For my daughters; you have endured so much over the last few years and having to endure this was beyond tough. You stepped up even in your own agony to do what was needed.

Fourth, I would like to thank my Lord and Savior, Jesus Christ. Though the event was terrible, he has allowed me to continue on this earth for a few more years and I am grateful for this.

Even though mentioned last, she is not. I would like to thank my wife for...Everything. How can I even do her justice by attempting to write down everything she means to me and everything she put herself through to save my life. It is impossible. I am very blessed to have a wife like her and I certainly hope you are inspired by her unfathomable faith. She is a modern day Shunammite woman (2 Kings Chapter 4).

21

SEARCHING FOR ANSWERS

The months after leaving the hospital were filled with efforts to heal, get stronger, and show my appreciation to the people who supported me. It was also a time to seek answers as to why I went into cardiac arrest on December 7.

While in the hospital, numerous tests were conducted with no definitive answers. When I first arrived to the hospital by ambulance, I was taken to the heart cath lab to check for blockages. Although no blockages were identified, I did have diminished blood flow in the lower ventricle. However, that particular blood vessel was naturally coiled in a way that they were not able to get a rod through to see if it was occluded—or obstructed. So, it is unclear if something happened in this area of my heart during the event to trigger the issue, but more than likely it did. By this time, my heart was beating normally, so no other intervention was required.

While I was unconscious in the ICU, a couple of CT scans of my coronary arteries (CTAs) were done. Once I moved to step down, an MRI was ordered. The day after the MRI, my cardiologist shared the results: scarring in my heart, consistent with a heart attack. This was an interesting find, but not an explanation as to why the scarring and heart attack had occurred. While this links to VFib and cardiac arrest, and probably happened at the same time, there was no clear explanation for why it happened. The usual culprit is a blockage, but there was none to be found.

After the internal defibrillator was in place, it was time to circle back on finding answers. I decided to get another cardiologist involved. He ordered a Cardiac Computed Tomography Angiography (CTA) and further blood tests. The CTA exam could identify plaque buildup in and around my heart. The blood tests were ordered to give an indication of a heightened risk of a heart attack. Both tests were inconclusive. Fortunately, I had no plaque in and around my heart— great news—but it did not explain what happened to me. So, I was left to wonder.

Speculations regarding inflammation around my heart and stress have been mentioned as playing a part, but nothing definitive. I have my own theories as well. It's troubling to think about. *How did I get into this position to start with and how do I prevent it from happening again?*

For three months after leaving the hospital, I battled the lung infection that started the day of my cardiac arrest. I worked with an infectious disease doctor to clear up the infection and I met with a pulmonologist to assess the condition and capacity of my lungs. I went through several breathing tests and CT scans and found that my lung capacity had taken a severe hit. Little by little, it improved. As the infection cleared up and I increased my aerobic activity, my lungs began to heal. It is a process that continues today; however, today my lungs have improved to a point that it does not limit my physical activity. I can now run and play sports. I am very thankful for that. Though my lungs are scarred and do not have the full capacity they once did, they are good enough for what I need.

The significant hearing loss in my right ear and, over time, my left ear is a mystery. I have seen numerous specialists in my own city, in other cities, and visited two hospitals in other states to determine if it might improve. It's a possibility that the lack of blood flow for 45 minutes during the cardiac arrest could have damaged some of the nerves in my inner ear. It's also possible that the heavy antibiotics I was on to treat my severe lung infection caused some hearing loss. Regardless, I am still on the search to find a way to restore some, if not all, of my hearing.

The last physical ailment after I left the hospital was a severe shoulder injury. The severity became apparent months after I returned home. My shoulder was probably already compromised before I entered the hospital due to years of playing ball and may have been injured further when I collapsed on December 7. It's also possible that since I was immobile for 18 days in the hospital and could not give feedback to the nurses, my shoulder could have been hurt further when I was moved around. I don't fault anyone, as I was not awake to inform folks of the pain. I even made it worse by attempting to play ball in the fall after leaving the hospital. Regardless, a year after leaving the hospital I had surgery to repair two fully torn rotator cuff tendons, a frayed bicep tendon, an inflamed bursa, and other damage.

Even though questions remain, I work on the things I can control and I pray for the things I cannot control. I pay a lot more attention to my body now. I check my blood pressure and have blood tests on a regular basis. I react to anything abnormal that may occur with my heart. I pay attention to stress and I eat properly...most of the time. I exercise...most of the time. I reduced my caffeine intake. I do the recommended things for someone who has been through what I have.

I guess this is similar to faith. You don't ever really know all the answers, but at some point, you have to move forward with what you do know. You have to reconcile that you will never know all the answers. Some things are a mystery and you have to be comfortable with that.

That is where I am with my belief and faith in God. I don't have all the answers to the questions that people will ask. I don't know why my brother passed away in the manner he did. I don't know why my sister-in-law was diagnosed with breast cancer and died in the manner she did. I don't know why my mother lived partially paralyzed for four years. However, there is enough evidence for the existence of God and enough evidence for the existence of a man named Jesus. I have to believe and be comfortable with the fact that I will not know every answer this side of Heaven, and neither will you. Maybe that is why I survived...just to tell you this.

22

BATTLING WITH THE DEVIL AND LEANING ON GOD

It is hard to really understand how I feel about what happened. The reality is, I was unconscious for most of the really stressful time. So, it is especially hard for me to wrap my mind around those early days in the hospital. God often reminds me of how dire the situation was and how much of a miracle it is that I am alive.

But sometimes, the devil casts doubt in my mind. *Did that really happen? Was it really a miracle that I survived? Maybe I was just lucky.* Then, if that is not enough, the devil starts to remind me of past failures or of ongoing issues. He tries to make me think I'm not special and that the miracle won't really make a difference. He tries to distract me.

I am susceptible to the devil's ploys. I recognize this, but it doesn't stop it from occurring. I am more attentive to these things now. However, there are times when the devil will haul me onto the mountain, like when he tempted Jesus (Matthew 4), and start pouring lies into my ears. And, at times, I allow it to go on for longer than I should.

Then, two words come to mind—But God. But God will

step in. But God will remind me that I am a miracle. But God will show me physical scars from my time in the hospital. But God will send someone—a friend, a neighbor, or a stranger to remind me that my recovery was no stroke of luck. But God will remind me that He is the source of truth.

A few months after returning home, I began sunrise walks again. It was my routine for a couple years before my cardiac arrest. I originally started these walks to vet all of life's frustrations to God. I prayed for the issues that impacted my family and asked God to fix them. When I resumed my walks, my approach was a little different. Now, most of the time, I ask God to lead and direct me and to fill me with his Holy Spirit. I ask him to give me wisdom, discernment, and strength.

It is no longer a pity party or an anger party as it had been before. Now, it is a time of charging the battery and looking for strength and power to move forward. More than ever, I am a target of the devil. He is not interested in you reading this book and he certainly isn't interested in me telling my story. So, every day, I need God's strength and the power that comes from the Holy Spirit to help me move forward with my mission.

The same is true of you. I am no different. You are also a miracle. If you are living and breathing and reading this book... you are a miracle. It is time for you to start viewing yourself in this manner. You have a story to tell and a mission to fulfill. The devil doesn't want you to fulfill either of these. He will do whatever it takes: Distract you. Lie to you. Frustrate you. Medicate you. Whatever it takes. But God. But God will save you from this daily. But only if you let him.

23

SIMPLIFY AND FOCUS

Over the span of five years, I sat in front of the six caskets of close family members. Knowing that I could have been the seventh dramatically changed my perspective. It narrowed my focus to what really matters and it eliminated the things that don't. However, this meant unpacking decisions I made in the past and looking for guidance for the future.

One thing I knew before my cardiac arrest and one thing I know for sure after is that our lives are too complicated. Most of the time we don't even realize it. We become used to the busyness and numb to the lives that we've built. They are usually built from the influences of outside sources: advertising, stores, peer pressure, you name it.

We acquire things without counting the cost. The time required to attain the money to buy the items. The time required to research the item. The time required to go out and actually purchase the item. The time required to move it around and maintain the item. The time required to attain the money to move around and maintain the item. The time required to clean the item. The time required to dispose of the item.

It has been said that the price of anything is the amount of life you are willing to trade for it. This also applies to commitments. We commit our time to TV shows, movies, video games, "take-your-time" social media platforms, and the list goes on and on. We fill our time with things that don't matter and we get frustrated because we don't have any time.

If you ask anyone at work how it's going, many will usually say they are slammed. Busy. If you dig deeper into their work routine, you will find it is filled with meetings, emails, and so on and so on. I have often said that meetings are a great opportunity to not get any work done. It is an opportunity to get updated and organized, but do not confuse it with actual work. I have also said that emails can be a distraction, as they show up unannounced and we often treat them as urgent items.

At the root of this, partially, is technology. Scandalous to say I know. Technology on one hand can make things easier, but most of the time, it makes things more complicated and confusing. We use it without weighing the cost.

Though I have known all of this for a number of years, once you lie in a hospital bed for 45 days, you become keenly aware of how you spend your time. As such, I have been on a journey to simplify my life and focus on the really important things. It has not been easy, but it's important to stay on it. It is difficult to unwind the life you have built when you recognize it is not the life you want.

I recently sat down and took a deep look into a number of major decisions I made in my life. I analyzed if, in the end, they were good decisions or bad decisions. Then I analyzed why I had made those decisions, drilling down to the key motivations. What I found were a few key elements. One was impatience. I was often in a hurry to make something happen. I wanted it now. Second, I was often driven by material acquisition—money and possessions. Third, I often listened to external sources–friends, books, media, etc. Oftentimes, when

I was motivated or influenced by those three factors, my decisions ended up being wrong. Some of them seriously wrong.

My theory is that the devil has a demon named Chaos. He has unleashed this demon into the world to drive us crazy. We listen to the influences of this demon and it makes our lives way more complicated than they should be. Often missing is the peace and freedom that comes when we are quiet, patient, still, and relying on God's guidance.

This mindset has driven me to simplify and really focus on what matters. But I do not do it alone. I have sought wisdom from God and trusted friends to continue to work toward the person I am meant to become. It is helpful to decide what is really at the core and important in life and focus on that. Eliminate the noise, the chaos, and the distractions that keep you from fulfilling the mission that resides in each one of us.

As I have unpacked all that has happened in my life, I realize that the one non-renewable resource is our time on earth. It is finite. Healthy habits and a little bit of God's grace might extend it, but in the end, our time on earth will end. However, our impact on other people's lives is renewable. It can span generations.

Focus on the things you can control and pray about the things you cannot. Constantly weigh how you exchange the non-renewable resource of your time. Slow down, be quiet, and seek God's wisdom and direction. Be really intentional. I now strive for these things on a daily basis. I encourage you to do the same.

24

PROBABILITIES

I should calculate the probability of my survival and recovery. This thought came to mind a few days after returning home. As time has passed, bit by bit, I have learned more about the first few weeks in the hospital. Some folks have labeled me a miracle. I have calculated the probability of that a few times and it is subjective. Others may calculate it a little differently, but regardless, there are many pieces and factors that went into figuring it out.

The first is the probability that Amy was home when I went into cardiac arrest. That morning, she had taken our niece to school and stopped by the grocery store to pick up two items. While there, she didn't run into anyone who would have engaged in conversation with her and she didn't browse the aisles. Had either of these two things occurred, she would have been delayed getting home. Even a stop at an additional traffic light would have delayed her arrival. Within five minutes of her returning home, I went into cardiac arrest. What is the probability that she was not delayed?

Within minutes of me passing out on the bathroom floor and going into cardiac arrest, Amy called our neighbor, Joye. Even in her shock, Amy remembered that Joye was a nurse.

It was early in the morning, but Joye answered the phone. As soon as Joye heard Amy's cry for help, she ran across our lawns barefoot and in her pajamas. As soon as Joye entered our home and saw me, she immediately began CPR. This saved my life and is most certainly the reason I do not have brain damage. What is the probability that in her shock, Amy would remember to call Joye, that Joye was home, and she would respond so quickly?

While Joye worked to save my life, her husband, Jack, called 911. Within four minutes, the first paramedic arrived and two more were right behind in an ambulance that was already en route only a couple traffic lights away from our neighborhood. They were moments away from driving in the opposite direction to another EMS location. Had the 911 call been delayed even thirty seconds, the paramedics would have been headed in the opposite direction. What is the probability that three paramedics arrived so quickly and took over CPR for Joye who was already exhausted?

Shortly after, two different fire stations were dispatched to our home. The call had come in at shift change so they had not begun their normal duties and were able to respond faster. Included in this group was another paramedic. Though the probability of their quick response is high, it is a probability that needs to be factored.

All total, a dozen individuals were in our home within minutes. Paramedics and firefighters diligently worked on me for well over 30 minutes. They utilized medicine and six defibrillator paddle shocks to establish a normal heartbeat. But I was without a regular heartbeat for approximately 45 minutes. What is the probability that they would get a heartbeat after six shocks from the defibrillator? What is the probability that they would not stop trying after five shocks?

Our subdivision is right across the street from a good

hospital. I can ride my bike there in 10 minutes. However, as good of a hospital as it is, it was not adequately prepared to treat my situation. Had I been taken there, I may not have survived the day. The paramedics asked Amy if they could take me 25 minutes down the road to MUSC. She agreed. Even though the paramedics knew this was the best choice, there was a possibility they could have taken me to the nearest hospital, which would have delayed proper treatment. Though high, what is the probability of them taking me straight to MUSC?

When I arrived at MUSC, questions surrounded my cardiac arrest. Was it a stroke or a heart attack? With Amy's information, I was sent to the heart cath lab to check for blockages in one of my coronary arteries. Though doctors did not find any, they did discover diminished flow in the lower left ventricle of my heart. This led them to believe that this may have been the origin of events. This information was important for the next few decisions. Again, though high, what is the probability they would make the right call this early in my arrival?

Within a couple of hours, my lung function suffered. I had vomited and aspirated my breakfast into my lungs, and they were unresponsive. Though my heart was beating now, my body was shutting down. The doctors tried everything. After a number of different approaches, they made a last recommendation to Amy—life support to act as a heart and lung machine by extracting blood out of the body, oxygenating it and returning it to the body. Many people in dire need of this machine ultimately do not survive. However, without this machine, I most certainly would not have survived. Only a few hospitals have this device—MUSC happened to be one. What is the probability that I would be taken to a hospital with an ECMO?

The ECMO had an entry point located in my neck and an exit point located on the inside of my thigh. After a few days on the machine, I developed an external bleed at the cannulas site on my neck. Blood began oozing from the site and it could not be stopped. I received extra blood to make up for the external bleed. They couldn't gain control of the external bleed; however, my condition improved enough to take me off of ECMO. What is the probability of having an external bleed, receiving blood transfusions, and still improving?

I was on heavy doses of heparin to prevent blood clots and to lessen the possibility of a stroke. However, in the course of this, I developed an internal lower GI bleed. Not only was I bleeding externally, I was also bleeding internally. A risky decision was made to discontinue the use of heparin to help stop the bleeding. In the end, I did not have a stroke and the bleeding stopped. What is the probability that these issues would not complicate my condition further and cause permanent damage, or even death?

Without a regular pulse for 45 minutes, I could have had collateral damage—severe brain damage or stroke due to the lack of oxygen. While on ECMO, I was attached to numerous monitors. At one point, the device that monitored brain activity showed very little response. The nurse on duty at that time turned off the monitor to not further discourage Amy. There was worry that I may have brain damage. I was not responding to any of the neurological checks. A scan revealed a minor stroke. It was only after I woke up that they determined I had no significant brain damage. What is the probability that through all of this trauma, my brain remained intact and that I did not incur major brain damage or experience a major stroke?

As mentioned, my lungs were in terrible shape. I developed a severe lung infection that remained for over four months. I was on powerful antibiotics to combat the infection. Even so, I developed a very high fever and my lungs needed time to heal.

At one point, the staff attempted to remove me from ECMO, but my lungs would not respond, leading me to remain on the machine for another week. Even more dire was the increased chance of contracting COVID. The risk became so great while I was in the ICU, that the hospital changed the visitation policy and restricted the number of people who could visit. If I had contracted COVID or any other respiratory disease, it may have been fatal. What is the probability that I would survive the infection, not contract COVID or other respiratory diseases like pneumonia, and walk out of the hospital?

Another issue I developed while in the ICU involved a blood clot in my left leg. Evidently, when working on proper circulation for the ECMO machine, an issue developed in a major vein in my left leg. After I woke up, I noticed a big knot on the inside of my left leg and it was pretty numb. In the end, it all worked out, but what is the probability that it could have gone the other way and caused a stroke or other complications?

A few days after getting home, I thought through all of these scenarios and their probabilities. I have since gained an even greater understanding of each of these situations. To get an overall probability of survival and recovery, I multiplied all the individual probabilities together. This is very subjective, and if you run the numbers, we would probably arrive at different conclusions. However, I think we would find that even though our numbers may be different, the improbability of survival and recovery would be significant. In fact, I think it would be so significant, that it may lead you to pause and wonder if this was luck or not. I calculated it a few times. Each time I did, the probability of survival was so small that I would have had a better chance at winning the Powerball lottery, which currently has a probability of 1 in 292 million.

Then, if you factor in the probability of me writing a book and you reading this far into the book, what are the chances that all of this is just a mere coincidence? I do not think it is. Many people have called my survival and recovery a miracle. I will leave that to you to decide. But the fact of the matter is, if you are reading this, you are involved in something rare. And that should make you pause and think.

25

OWNING A MIRACLE

It seems like everyone knows something miraculous occurred in my life. As the previous chapter mentioned, the odds were stacked against me, and I survived anyway—and now I am looked at differently.

"If you could have seen what I saw, and then see you today, your faith would certainly grow," Joye said. She is a very analytical person. Very black and white. Even she had to pause and wonder if something miraculous did happen.

In the months after I returned home, my interactions with people reminded me of how special my survival and recovery was. As I saw people I knew, their faces lit up with joy, and they talked about how diligent they prayed and how miraculous my survival had been. I met several people who did not know me previously, but who had prayed for me—a confirmation of their belief in prayer.

It was hard for me to grasp. In a certain way, I had just been along for the ride. For 18 days, I was unconscious and unaware of my situation. For a few days after waking up, I had no concept of anything. In reality, it was several months before I became aware of most of the story. So, when people called me a miracle, I honestly didn't know how to respond. It was strange being called that. And, it was hard to own it.

A miracle is defined as a surprising and welcome event that is not explicable by natural or scientific laws and is therefore considered the work of a divine agency. How could this have been bestowed upon me? The actual event, a cardiac arrest, was a terrible event. But the survival and recovery...could it really be a miracle? *How am I deserving of such a miracle? What do I do with it?*

I have had these thoughts and to be honest, at times, I still have them today. Over four years later, people remind me of how improbable my survival was and they call me a miracle. I struggle to process that. I smile and thank them for their prayers. Even though I have done the probability calculation, and the significance of that improbable number has sunk in, I still wonder why.

As time has passed though, I have heard many stories about how folks' faith has increased because of my story, leading them to pray, to hope, and to see something good happen in the midst of many bad things in the world. It gives them hope, that sometimes, things do work out here on earth for good. And with that, they believe. Even people who may not have believed in God before, now believe that something not of this earth occurred. So, when they see me alive and well, it reminds them of their faith and belief.

However, it is easy to return to the old life and forget. The world has a way of distracting us, of keeping us busy and tied up in the issues of today. Our world is filled with such things...distractions. And it is a very large magnet. But in the end, those things really do not matter. Even more today, I desire a simpler life. One that is free of worldly distractions, one that makes deposits into people's lives and eternity. The response to my event was unbelievable. People came together to support Amy and the girls. People came together to pray for my survival and recovery. People came together to save my life here on earth. The challenge for all of us is to replicate that to others in need.

Amy reflected on the toughest years of our lives, and it came down to God and the people who helped us make it through. "Be there for people. Just show up. You do not have to have the right words. Just a hug speaks volumes. Have faith and hope. Believe and pray for a miracle. God does not always answer our prayers the way we hope. I know that too well from our own losses. I watched my 49-year-old sister die of metastatic breast cancer two months before Kevin went into cardiac arrest. Spend time and savor the times you have with those you love. We will all have hard times in this life until we get to Heaven. But remember: believers always have God to lean on. This was hands down the toughest event of my life. Losing our moms, Kevin's brother and my sister were tough, but I had Kevin by my side then. I could not imagine life without him. The miracle God performed in Kevin was more than keeping Kevin with our family. The miracle spoke life in our faith, made believers out of unbelievers, and showed medical staff and believers that God still performs miracles."

I carry the story of a terrible event that turned into a remarkable event. I now have the responsibility to tell my story. Not for my glory, but for His. A reminder that ordinary people stepped up in faith and they were rewarded for their faithfulness. A reminder that even though many things do not work out here on earth like we want, sometimes it does. And we should persevere in this hope. Hope for a better tomorrow. Hope for eternity.

26

NEVER GIVE UP

A few years ago, my daughter spent a week in Togo, West Africa on a missions trip with our church. When she returned and told us about the trip, I asked her one question, "What did you bring back with you?" She referred to a few souvenirs, but I stopped her. I wasn't asking about material items. I wanted to know what she brought back inside of her. She simply stated "joy." She witnessed the joy of the people in Togo despite not having many material items. She wanted that.

My hope is that you bring something back after reading this book, that you will see more to life than some of the things our world offers. My hope is that this book inspires you to seek the things that really matter—relationships, investing in people, joy, and faith in God. My hope is that if you are struggling with anything, that you too will raise up a group of prayer warriors to see you through.

At the beginning of the book, I stated who I wrote this book for—the confused, the lost, the discouraged. If that is you, I hope that this book has inspired you to seek the one who can provide strength, hope, peace, and encouragement in a chaotic and broken world; Our Lord and Savior Jesus Christ.

Over time, I have had the opportunity to reflect quite a bit on this experience. One thing that is evident, although I already knew this—God is definitely real. He still heals and He still performs miracles. However, this isn't a story about me. It is a story about you. You may be one of many who prayed for my survival and recovery. This is about you and the impact this has had on your life, your faithfulness, and your faith. I encourage you to go to God with your hurts, your pain, and your despair, but do not do it in a vacuum. Do it with the Body of Christ. Because this is how we do it. Together.

I have so many thoughts and have learned so many lessons since my cardiac arrest. Two final ones stand out as I write this final chapter. For those who are enduring the struggle, whatever it is, many people will come alongside you. They will be there to pray for you, cry with you, laugh with you, and be with you. This is so precious and valuable. This is my experience and I am so humbled and thankful for everyone who prayed, cried, laughed, and sat with us. In the end, however, no one will fully understand your struggle here on earth like the great Healer does. God wants to walk with you on this journey of healing, but only if you let him.

Second, I am reminded that most of our struggles are spiritual in nature. Not all, but most. What we cannot do is reconcile spiritual issues through human earthly means. Spiritual issues must be dealt with through our Father in Heaven. As we continue on our healing journey, or work through our struggles, we must turn our eyes and hearts over to the great Healer who wants more than anything to pray with you, cry with you, laugh with you, and be with you.

Remember, God has not given up on you. God loves you. He is not going to give up on you, no matter what.

"When thou passest through the waters, I *will be* with thee; and through the rivers, they shall not overflow thee: when thou walkest through the fire, thou shalt not be burned; neither shall the flame kindle upon thee."

Isaiah 43:2 (KJV)

ABOUT THE AUTHOR

Kevin Strader is an engineer by trade, one who enjoys solving problems. But in 2021, when a sudden cardiac arrest nearly took his life, he faced a problem he couldn't fix on his own. That experience inspired him to write about his survival and recovery, sharing the miracles of prayer and the hope and gratitude he found in the community that helped save his life here on earth. Kevin is married to his wife, Amy, and they reside in Charleston, South Carolina. Together, they have two daughters, Caroline and Reagan. He enjoys sports, traveling, and being intentional with the things that truly matter—relationships, investing in people, joy, and faith in God.